The United States of AMERICA

A State-by-State Guide

Millie Miller & Cyndi Nelson

SCHOLASTIC REFERENCE

An imprint of

SCHOLASTIC

Acknowledgments

Thank you, Ivan and Scott, our enduring husbands and critics.
Tell the kids—Scott, Jon, Tyler, Peter, Jeffrey, and Stina—that we'll be home for dinner.

Special thanks for valuable input to:

Audrey Benedict (Cloud Ridge Naturalists), Brad Easterson (American PIE—Public Information on the Environment), Nancy Laties Feresten (Senior Editor, Scholastic Inc.), Barbara French (Bat Conservation International), Steve Frye and Scott Severs (Boulder Wild Bird Center), Laurie Lanzen Harris (Editor of *Biography Today*, Omnigraphics, Inc.), Boris Kondratieff (Ft. Collins Entomology Department), Chris Pague (The Nature Conservancy), Gerry Roehm (The U.S. Fish and Wildlife Service), Nancy Sabato (Art Director, Scholastic Inc.), Judy Volc (Children's Literature Specialist, Boulder Public Library), Katherine Young and Fran Grzenda (Foothill Elementary Librarians, Boulder, CO), all the folks at Scholastic Inc. who made this project possible, and the many people throughout the U.S.A. who answered our endless questions.

Additional thanks to our support team:

Dr. John Carter (southern gentleman), Ginny Gardner (our Hawaiian connection), Bill and Lyn Gullette (Endaba, Pagosa Springs B&B), Marcy Lockhart (world traveler and teacher), Jake Lucas (resident Montana expert), Carl Mackey (Plant Ecologist, Rocky Mountain Arsenal National Wildlife Refuge), Marilyn Marinelli (educator extraordinaire), Walt and Velma Nelson (grandparents), and Ana Sanjuan (steadfast source of encouragement and nourishment).

Population statistics for the 50 states, Washington, D.C., and Puerto Rico are from the U.S. Cenus Bureau's July 1, 2004 Population Estimates (www.census.gov).

★　　★　　★　　★

ISBN 0-439-82765-5

12 11 10 9 8 7 6 5 4 3 2 1   06 07 08 09 10

Printed in the U.S.A.   14

This edition paperback printing, October 2006

Book design by Nancy Sabato
Composition by BNGO Books/Kevin Callahan

Dedicated to the
Children of the World

"The survival of
the world depends
upon our sharing what
we have and
working together."

— Frank Fools Crow,
Teton Sioux

The U.S.–Canadian Border is the longest undefended border in the world.

CANADA

WASHINGTON

OREGON

Cascade Mountains

IDAHO

Missouri River

MONTANA

NORTH DAKO

WYOMING

Continental Divide

Rocky

SOUTH DAKOTA

NEBRASKA

Sierra Nevada Mountains

Pacific Ocean

NEVADA

UTAH

Mountains

COLORADO

KANSAS

CALIFORNIA

Colorado River

Death Valley is the lowest spot in the nation, at 282 feet below sea level.

ARIZONA

NEW MEXICO

National bird: Bald eagle

The northernmost point in the U.S.A. is Point Barrow, AK.

MEXICO

Rio Grande

TEXAS

Each year, it rains about 460 inches on the wettest place in the world, Mt. Waialeale, Kauai.

ALASKA

HAWAII

Cape Wrangel, AK, is the westernmost point in the U.S.A.

Denali is the highest mountain in North America. It is 20,320 feet tall.

Ka Lae, HI, is the southernmost point in the U.S.A.

The United States of America was founded July 4, 1776. • Population: 293,655,404 • Area: 3,675,031 square miles

Lake Superior is the largest freshwater lake in the world.

The St. Lawrence Seaway is the longest canal in the world. It is about 450 miles long.

The easternmost point in the U.S.A. is West Quoddy Head, ME.

CANADA

Lake Superior

MINNESOTA

MICHIGAN

Lake Huron

WISCONSIN

Lake Michigan

MICHIGAN

Lake Ontario

St. Lawrence River

MAINE

VERMONT

NEW HAMPSHIRE

NEW YORK

MASSACHUSETTS

RHODE ISLAND

CONNECTICUT

Lake Erie

PENNSYLVANIA

NEW JERSEY

IOWA

ILLINOIS

INDIANA

OHIO

DELAWARE

MARYLAND

WASHINGTON, D.C.

Ohio River

WEST VIRGINIA

Appalachian Mountains

VIRGINIA

Mississippi River

Missouri River

MISSOURI

KENTUCKY

TENNESSEE

NORTH CAROLINA

OKLAHOMA

ARKANSAS

SOUTH CAROLINA

Atlantic Ocean

Extinct: Carolina parakeet. Over 250 U.S. plants and animals have disappeared since 1980.

MISSISSIPPI

ALABAMA

GEORGIA

LOUISIANA

FLORIDA

The Mississippi River is 2,348 miles long. It is the longest river in North America.

Gulf of Mexico

Puerto Rico is a U.S. commonwealth and located about 1,000 miles southeast of Miami.

PUERTO RICO

National flower: Rose

THE UNITED STATES OF AMERICA

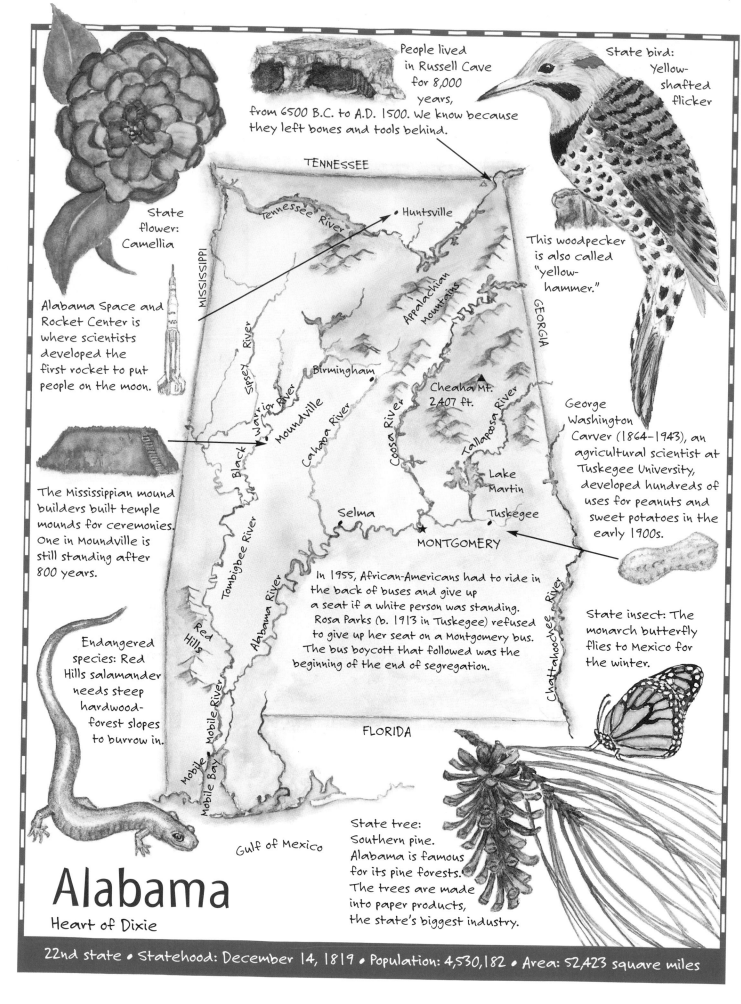

People lived in Russell Cave for 8,000 years, from 6500 B.C. to A.D. 1500. We know because they left bones and tools behind.

State bird: Yellow-shafted flicker

This woodpecker is also called "yellow-hammer."

State flower: Camellia

Alabama Space and Rocket Center is where scientists developed the first rocket to put people on the moon.

The Mississippian mound builders built temple mounds for ceremonies. One in Moundville is still standing after 800 years.

George Washington Carver (1864–1943), an agricultural scientist at Tuskegee University, developed hundreds of uses for peanuts and sweet potatoes in the early 1900s.

Endangered species: Red Hills salamander needs steep hardwood-forest slopes to burrow in.

In 1955, African-Americans had to ride in the back of buses and give up a seat if a white person was standing. Rosa Parks (b. 1913 in Tuskegee) refused to give up her seat on a Montgomery bus. The bus boycott that followed was the beginning of the end of segregation.

State insect: The monarch butterfly flies to Mexico for the winter.

TENNESSEE
MISSISSIPPI
Tennessee River
Huntsville
Appalachian Mountains
GEORGIA
Sipsey River
Birmingham
Warrior River
Moundville
Cahaba River
Black
Cheaha Mt. 2,407 ft.
Coosa River
Tallapoosa River
Lake Martin
Tuskegee
Selma
MONTGOMERY
Tombigbee River
Alabama River
Red Hills
Chattahoochee River
FLORIDA
Mobile River
Mobile Bay
Mobile
Gulf of Mexico

State tree: Southern pine. Alabama is famous for its pine forests. The trees are made into paper products, the state's biggest industry.

Alabama
Heart of Dixie

22nd state • Statehood: December 14, 1819 • Population: 4,530,182 • Area: 52,423 square miles

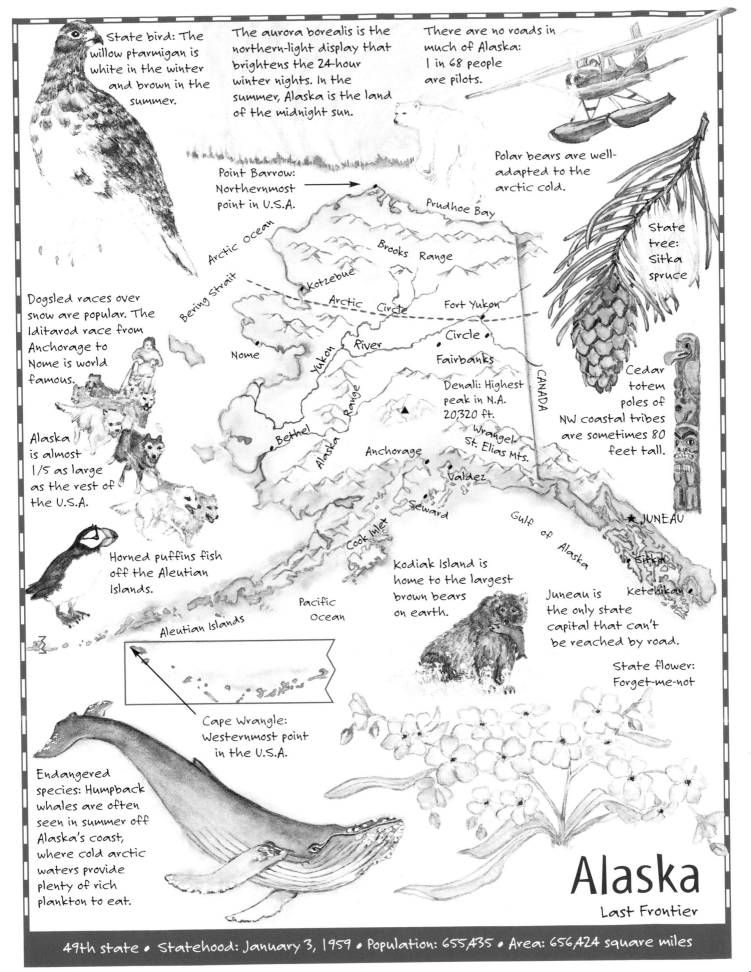

State bird: The willow ptarmigan is white in the winter and brown in the summer.

The aurora borealis is the northern-light display that brightens the 24-hour winter nights. In the summer, Alaska is the land of the midnight sun.

There are no roads in much of Alaska: 1 in 68 people are pilots.

Polar bears are well-adapted to the arctic cold.

Point Barrow: Northernmost point in U.S.A.

Prudhoe Bay

Arctic Ocean

Brooks Range

State tree: Sitka spruce

Bering Strait

Kotzebue

Arctic Circle

Fort Yukon

Dogsled races over snow are popular. The Iditarod race from Anchorage to Nome is world famous.

Nome

Yukon River

Circle

Fairbanks

Denali: Highest peak in N.A. 20,320 ft.

CANADA

Cedar totem poles of NW coastal tribes are sometimes 80 feet tall.

Alaska is almost 1/5 as large as the rest of the U.S.A.

Bethel

Alaska Range

Anchorage

Wrangel-St. Elias Mts.

Valdez

Seward

Gulf of Alaska

JUNEAU

Sitka

Ketchikan

Cook Inlet

Horned puffins fish off the Aleutian Islands.

Aleutian Islands

Pacific Ocean

Kodiak Island is home to the largest brown bears on earth.

Juneau is the only state capital that can't be reached by road.

Cape Wrangle: Westernmost point in the U.S.A.

State flower: Forget-me-not

Endangered species: Humpback whales are often seen in summer off Alaska's coast, where cold arctic waters provide plenty of rich plankton to eat.

Alaska
Last Frontier

49th state • Statehood: January 3, 1959 • Population: 655,435 • Area: 656,424 square miles

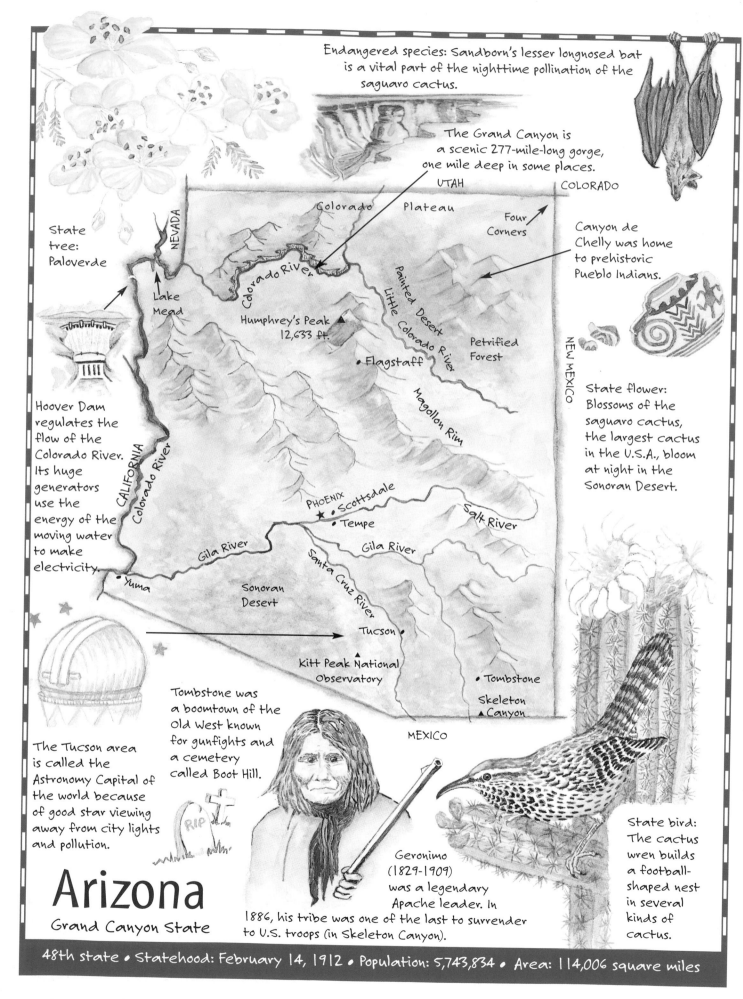

Endangered species: Sandborn's lesser longnosed bat is a vital part of the nighttime pollination of the saguaro cactus.

The Grand Canyon is a scenic 277-mile-long gorge, one mile deep in some places.

UTAH

COLORADO

Colorado Plateau

Four Corners

Canyon de Chelly was home to prehistoric Pueblo Indians.

State tree: Paloverde

NEVADA

Lake Mead

Colorado River

Humphrey's Peak 12,633 ft.

Painted Desert

Little Colorado River

Petrified Forest

Flagstaff

NEW MEXICO

State flower: Blossoms of the saguaro cactus, the largest cactus in the U.S.A., bloom at night in the Sonoran Desert.

Hoover Dam regulates the flow of the Colorado River. Its huge generators use the energy of the moving water to make electricity.

CALIFORNIA

Colorado River

Magollon Rim

PHOENIX
Scottsdale
Tempe

Salt River

Gila River

Gila River

Yuma

Sonoran Desert

Santa Cruz River

Tucson

Kitt Peak National Observatory

Tombstone

Skeleton Canyon

MEXICO

The Tucson area is called the Astronomy Capital of the world because of good star viewing away from city lights and pollution.

Tombstone was a boomtown of the Old West known for gunfights and a cemetery called Boot Hill.

RIP

Geronimo (1829-1909) was a legendary Apache leader. In 1886, his tribe was one of the last to surrender to U.S. troops (in Skeleton Canyon).

State bird: The cactus wren builds a football-shaped nest in several kinds of cactus.

Arizona
Grand Canyon State

48th state • Statehood: February 14, 1912 • Population: 5,743,834 • Area: 114,006 square miles

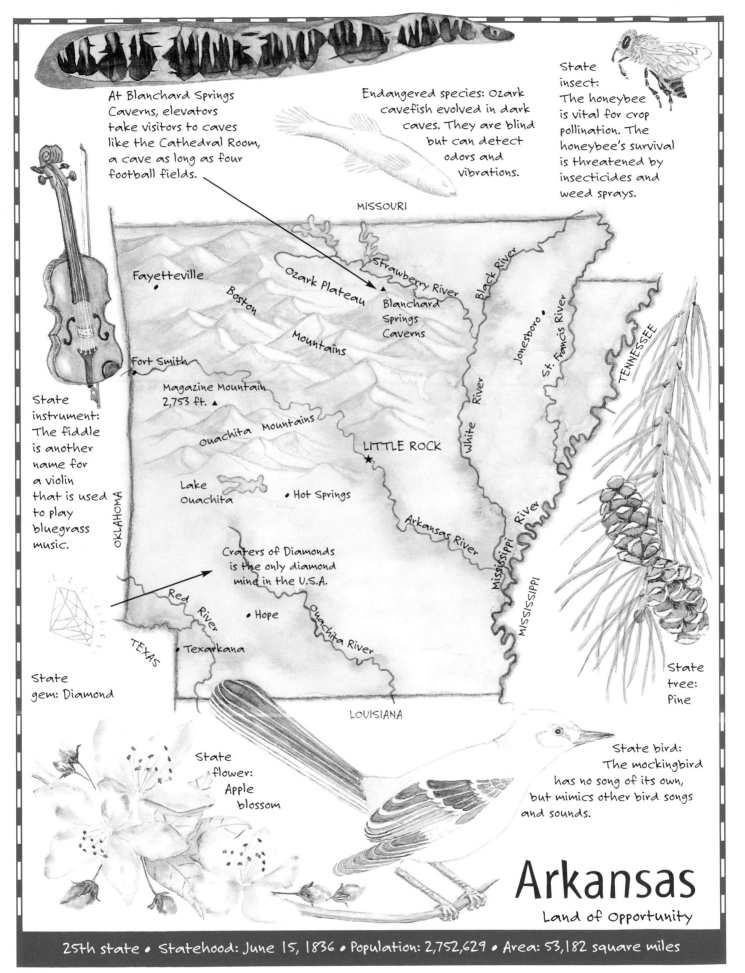

At Blanchard Springs Caverns, elevators take visitors to caves like the Cathedral Room, a cave as long as four football fields.

Endangered species: Ozark cavefish evolved in dark caves. They are blind but can detect odors and vibrations.

State insect: The honeybee is vital for crop pollination. The honeybee's survival is threatened by insecticides and weed sprays.

State instrument: The fiddle is another name for a violin that is used to play bluegrass music.

State gem: Diamond

Craters of Diamonds is the only diamond mine in the U.S.A.

State flower: Apple blossom

State tree: Pine

State bird: The mockingbird has no song of its own, but mimics other bird songs and sounds.

MISSOURI

Fayetteville
Ozark Plateau
Boston
Mountains
Strawberry River
Black River
Blanchard Springs Caverns
Jonesboro
St. Francis River
TENNESSEE

Fort Smith
Magazine Mountain 2,753 ft. ▲
Ouachita Mountains
White River
LITTLE ROCK

OKLAHOMA

Lake Ouachita
• Hot Springs
Arkansas River
Mississippi River

Red River
Hope
Ouachita River
MISSISSIPPI

TEXAS
• Texarkana

LOUISIANA

Arkansas
Land of Opportunity

25th state • Statehood: June 15, 1836 • Population: 2,752,629 • Area: 53,182 square miles

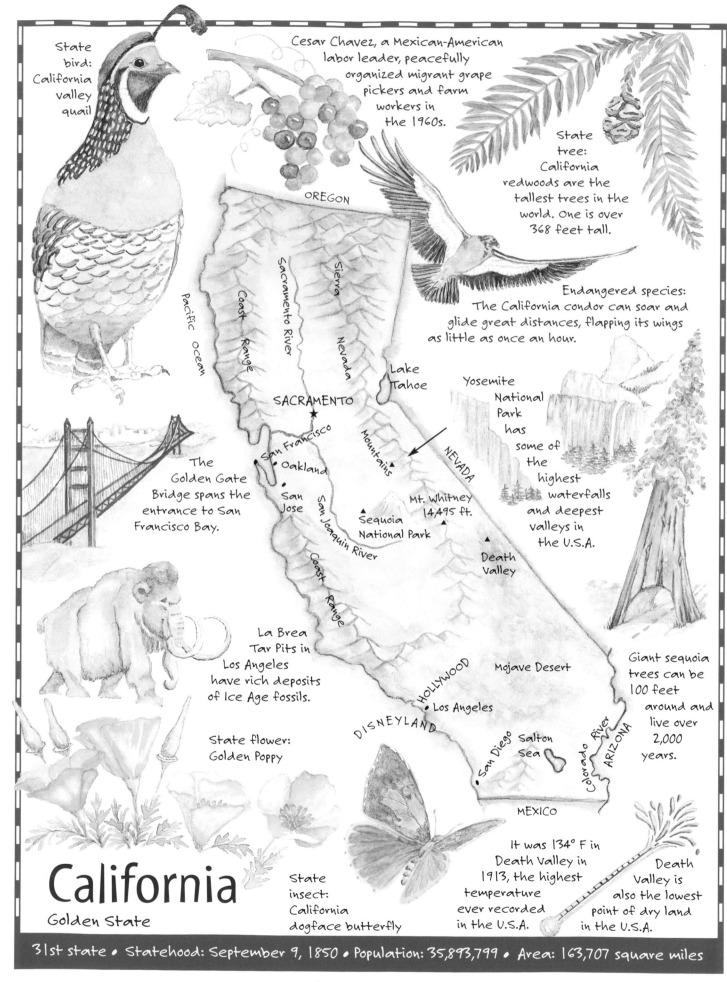

State bird: California valley quail

Cesar Chavez, a Mexican-American labor leader, peacefully organized migrant grape pickers and farm workers in the 1960s.

State tree: California redwoods are the tallest trees in the world. One is over 368 feet tall.

Endangered species: The California condor can soar and glide great distances, flapping its wings as little as once an hour.

OREGON

Coast Range

Sacramento River

Sierra Nevada

Pacific Ocean

Lake Tahoe

SACRAMENTO

San Francisco

Oakland

San Jose

Mountains

NEVADA

Yosemite National Park has some of the highest waterfalls and deepest valleys in the U.S.A.

The Golden Gate Bridge spans the entrance to San Francisco Bay.

San Joaquin River

Sequoia National Park

Mt. Whitney 14,495 ft.

Death Valley

La Brea Tar Pits in Los Angeles have rich deposits of Ice Age fossils.

Coast Range

Giant sequoia trees can be 100 feet around and live over 2,000 years.

State flower: Golden Poppy

HOLLYWOOD

Mojave Desert

Los Angeles

DISNEYLAND

San Diego

Salton Sea

Colorado River

ARIZONA

MEXICO

California
Golden State

State insect: California dogface butterfly

It was 134° F in Death Valley in 1913, the highest temperature ever recorded in the U.S.A.

Death Valley is also the lowest point of dry land in the U.S.A.

31st state • Statehood: September 9, 1850 • Population: 35,893,799 • Area: 163,707 square miles

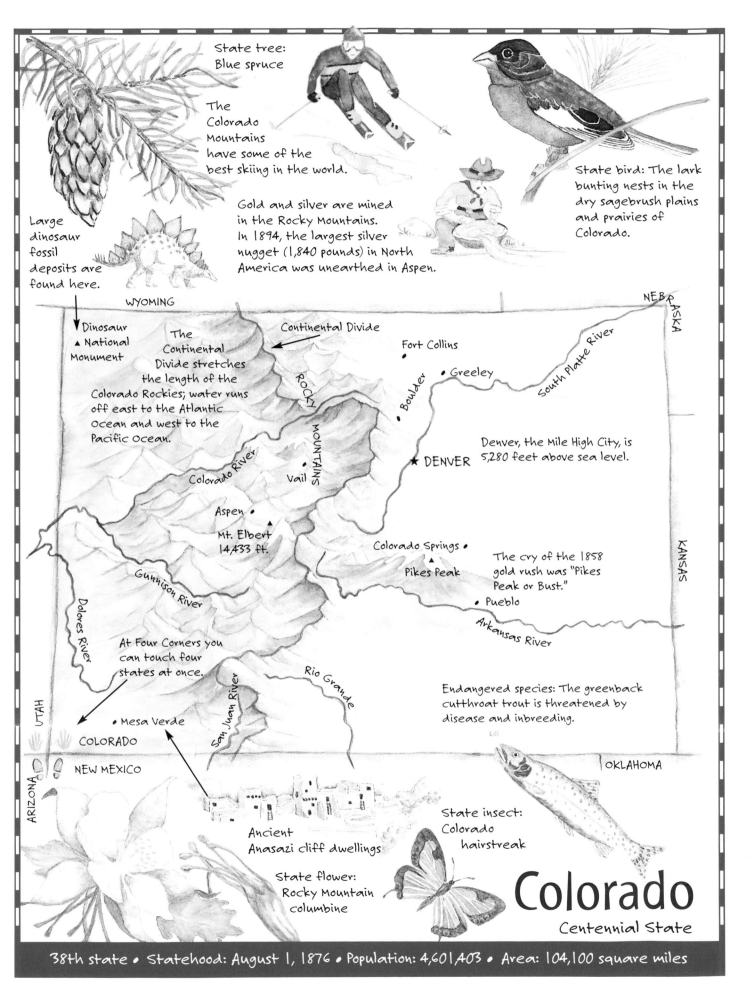

State tree:
Blue spruce

The Colorado Mountains have some of the best skiing in the world.

Gold and silver are mined in the Rocky Mountains. In 1894, the largest silver nugget (1,840 pounds) in North America was unearthed in Aspen.

State bird: The lark bunting nests in the dry sagebrush plains and prairies of Colorado.

Large dinosaur fossil deposits are found here.

WYOMING

Dinosaur ▲ National Monument

The Continental Divide stretches the length of the Colorado Rockies; water runs off east to the Atlantic Ocean and west to the Pacific Ocean.

Continental Divide

ROCKY MOUNTAINS

Colorado River

Vail

Aspen •
▲ Mt. Elbert
14,433 ft.

Gunnison River

Dolores River

At Four Corners you can touch four states at once.

• Mesa Verde

San Juan River

Rio Grande

UTAH

COLORADO

ARIZONA

NEW MEXICO

Fort Collins
•

Boulder • Greeley

South Platte River

★ DENVER

Denver, the Mile High City, is 5,280 feet above sea level.

Colorado Springs •

▲ Pikes Peak

The cry of the 1858 gold rush was "Pikes Peak or Bust."

• Pueblo

Arkansas River

KANSAS

Endangered species: The greenback cutthroat trout is threatened by disease and inbreeding.

OKLAHOMA

NEBRASKA

Ancient Anasazi cliff dwellings

State insect: Colorado hairstreak

State flower: Rocky Mountain columbine

Colorado
Centennial State

38th state • Statehood: August 1, 1876 • Population: 4,601,403 • Area: 104,100 square miles

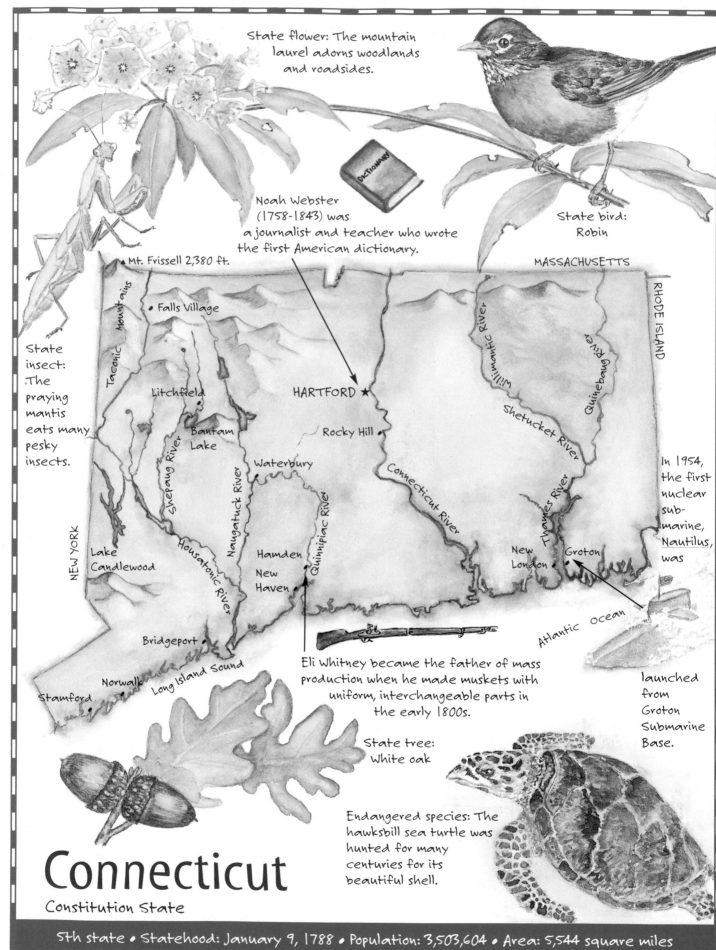

State flower: The mountain laurel adorns woodlands and roadsides.

State bird: Robin

Noah Webster (1758-1843) was a journalist and teacher who wrote the first American dictionary.

State insect: The praying mantis eats many pesky insects.

Mt. Frissell 2,380 ft.

MASSACHUSETTS

RHODE ISLAND

Taconic Mountains

• Falls Village

Litchfield

Bantam Lake

Shepaug River

Naugatuck River

HARTFORD ★

Rocky Hill •

Waterbury

Quinnipiac River

Willimantic River

Quinebaug River

Shetucket River

Connecticut River

Thames River

In 1954, the first nuclear sub-marine, Nautilus, was

NEW YORK

Lake Candlewood

Housatonic River

Hamden

New Haven •

New London

Groton

Atlantic Ocean

launched from Groton Submarine Base.

Bridgeport

Norwalk

Stamford

Long Island Sound

Eli Whitney became the father of mass production when he made muskets with uniform, interchangeable parts in the early 1800s.

State tree: White oak

Endangered species: The hawksbill sea turtle was hunted for many centuries for its beautiful shell.

Connecticut
Constitution State

5th state • Statehood: January 9, 1788 • Population: 3,503,604 • Area: 5,544 square miles

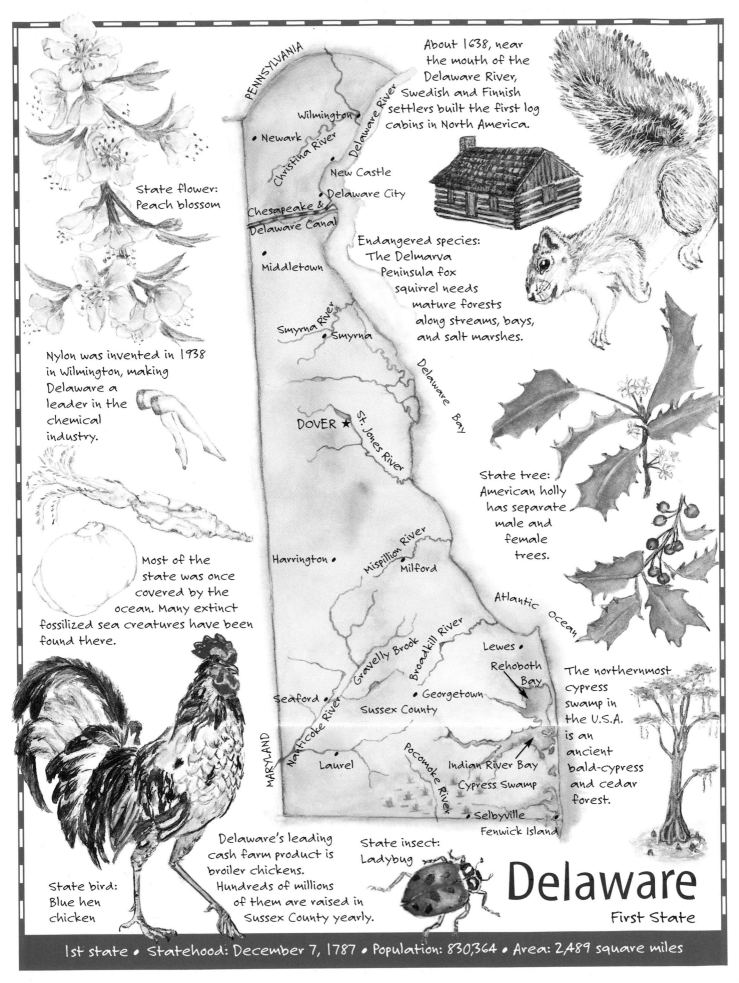

State flower: Peach blossom

Nylon was invented in 1938 in Wilmington, making Delaware a leader in the chemical industry.

Most of the state was once covered by the ocean. Many extinct fossilized sea creatures have been found there.

State bird: Blue hen chicken

Delaware's leading cash farm product is broiler chickens. Hundreds of millions of them are raised in Sussex County yearly.

PENNSYLVANIA

Wilmington
Newark
Christina River
Delaware River
New Castle
Delaware City
Chesapeake & Delaware Canal
Middletown
Smyrna River
Smyrna
DOVER ★
St. Jones River
Delaware Bay
Harrington
Mispillion River
Milford
Gravelly Brook
Broadkill River
Lewes
Rehoboth Bay
Atlantic Ocean
Seaford
Nanticoke River
Georgetown
Sussex County
MARYLAND
Laurel
Pocomoke River
Indian River Bay
Cypress Swamp
Selbyville
Fenwick Island

About 1638, near the mouth of the Delaware River, Swedish and Finnish settlers built the first log cabins in North America.

Endangered species: The Delmarva Peninsula fox squirrel needs mature forests along streams, bays, and salt marshes.

State tree: American holly has separate male and female trees.

The northernmost cypress swamp in the U.S.A. is an ancient bald-cypress and cedar forest.

State insect: Ladybug

Delaware
First State

1st state • Statehood: December 7, 1787 • Population: 830,364 • Area: 2,489 square miles

State insect: Giant swallowtail butterfly

State flower: Orange blossom

State bird: Mockingbird

Florida grows 80% of the nation's oranges and grapefruits.

ALABAMA

Perdido River

Pensacola

GEORGIA

★ TALLAHASSEE

Apalachicola River

St. Mary's River

Jacksonville

Suwannee River

Gulf of Mexico

Apalachicola

Gainesville

St. John's River

The oldest European settlement in North America was founded at St. Augustine in 1565.

Daytona Beach

Pensacola Naval Air Station is home to the Blue Angels, the Navy's famous aerobatic team.

Lake George

Near Orlando are Epcot Center and Walt Disney World.

Orlando

Kissimmee

Cape Canaveral launches the space shuttle.

State tree: Sabal palm

Florida has more "champions," or largest living tree specimens, than any other state.

Tampa

St. Petersburg

Tampa Bay

Florida waters have more kinds of fish than any other place in the world.

Sarasota

Lake Okeechobee

Wild flamingos are now extinct in Florida.

Captiva Island

Sanibel Island

Ft. Lauderdale

The Everglades

Miami

Atlantic Ocean

Florida Keys—150-mile chain of small islands connected by highway.

Endangered species: The Florida manatee, a gentle "sea cow," cannot swim fast enough to avoid boat propellers near coasts.

Key Largo

Key West

Sunken treasures found here.

Florida

Sunshine State

27th state • Statehood: March 3, 1845 • Population: 17,397,161 • Area: 65,756 square miles

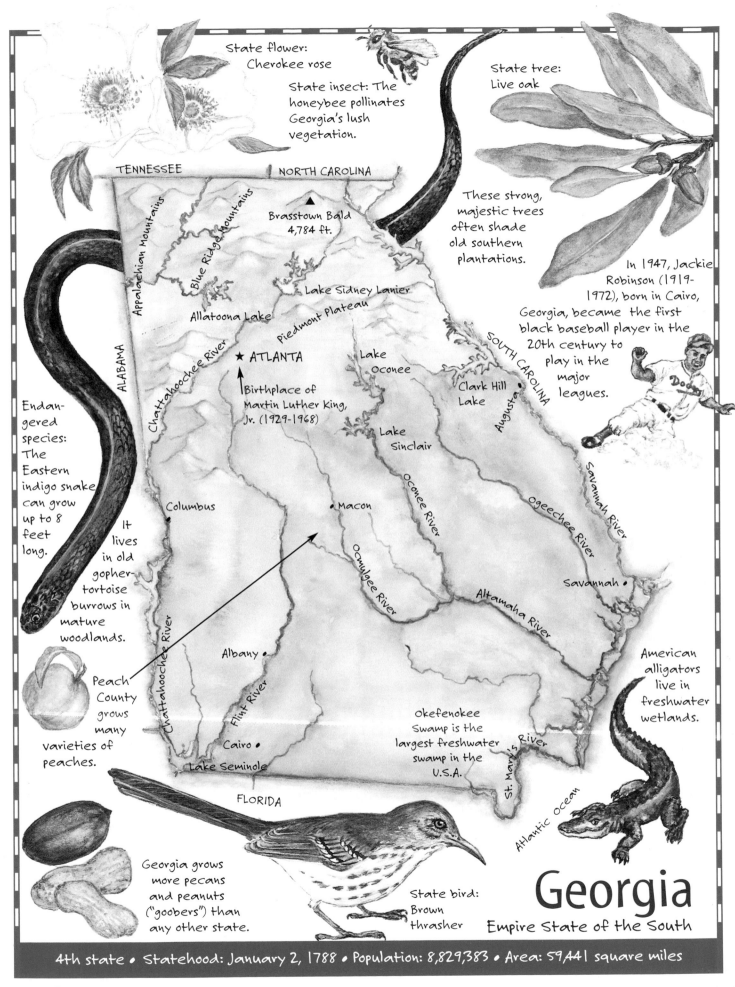

State flower: Cherokee rose

State insect: The honeybee pollinates Georgia's lush vegetation.

State tree: Live oak

These strong, majestic trees often shade old southern plantations.

In 1947, Jackie Robinson (1919-1972), born in Cairo, Georgia, became the first black baseball player in the 20th century to play in the major leagues.

TENNESSEE

NORTH CAROLINA

Appalachian Mountains

Blue Ridge Mountains

Brasstown Bald 4,784 ft.

Lake Sidney Lanier

Allatoona Lake

Piedmont Plateau

ALABAMA

Chattahoochee River

★ ATLANTA

Birthplace of Martin Luther King, Jr. (1929-1968)

Lake Oconee

SOUTH CAROLINA

Clark Hill Lake

Augusta

Lake Sinclair

Oconee River

Savannah River

Endangered species: The Eastern indigo snake can grow up to 8 feet long.

It lives in old gopher-tortoise burrows in mature woodlands.

Columbus

Macon

ogeechee River

Savannah

Ocmulgee River

Altamaha River

Peach County grows many varieties of peaches.

Chattahoochee River

Albany

Flint River

Cairo

American alligators live in freshwater wetlands.

Okefenokee Swamp is the largest freshwater swamp in the U.S.A.

St. Mary's River

Lake Seminole

FLORIDA

Atlantic Ocean

Georgia grows more pecans and peanuts ("goobers") than any other state.

State bird: Brown thrasher

Georgia
Empire State of the South

4th state • Statehood: January 2, 1788 • Population: 8,829,383 • Area: 59,441 square miles

The Hawaiian alphabet has 12 letters:
AEHIKLMNOPUW.
"Aloha" means both "hello"
and "good-bye."

This mountain is the wettest place on earth. It has an average annual rainfall of 460 inches.

State tree: Kukui tree

State flower: Yellow hibiscus

NIIHAU

KAUAI
▲ Mt. Waialeale

Pacific Ocean

"Hula" means "dance" in Hawaiian. Each dance tells a story.

The Hawaiian Islands were formed by volcanoes. Some are still active.

OAHU
Pearl Harbor
Kailua
HONOLULU

Pacific Ocean

MOLOKAI

LANAI
Lahaina
MAUI
KAHOOLAWE
Haleakala Crater

Home of the largest pineapple plantation in the world.

Whales winter in Hawaii's warm waters.

State bird: The Nene, an island goose, is now rare.

Surfing, the oldest sport in the U.S.A., started in Hawaii long before Columbus sailed.

Mauna Kea 13,796 ft.
Hilo
HAWAII

Pacific Ocean

Queen Liliuokalani (1838-1917) was the last of Hawaii's royalty to live in the only palace in the U.S.A.

Ka Lae: southernmost point in the U.S.A.

Endangered species: Hawaiian monk seals find a safe home in an island wildlife refuge.

Hawaii
Aloha State

50th state • Statehood: August 21, 1959 • Population: 1,262,840 • Area: 10,932 square miles

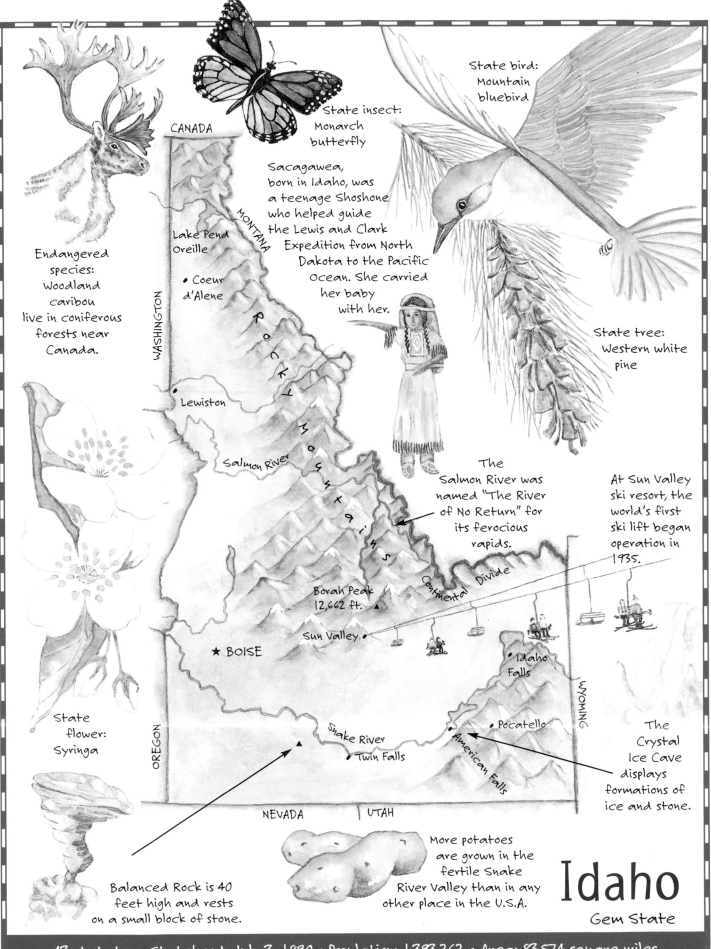

State insect: Monarch butterfly

State bird: Mountain bluebird

Sacagawea, born in Idaho, was a teenage Shoshone who helped guide the Lewis and Clark Expedition from North Dakota to the Pacific Ocean. She carried her baby with her.

State tree: Western white pine

CANADA

MONTANA

Lake Pend Oreille

• Coeur d'Alene

WASHINGTON

Rocky Mountains

• Lewiston

Salmon River

The Salmon River was named "The River of No Return" for its ferocious rapids.

At Sun Valley ski resort, the world's first ski lift began operation in 1935.

Continental Divide

Borah Peak 12,662 ft. ▲

Sun Valley •

★ BOISE

• Idaho Falls

WYOMING

Endangered species: Woodland caribou live in coniferous forests near Canada.

OREGON

Snake River

Twin Falls

• Pocatello

American Falls

The Crystal Ice Cave displays formations of ice and stone.

State flower: Syringa

NEVADA   UTAH

Balanced Rock is 40 feet high and rests on a small block of stone.

More potatoes are grown in the fertile Snake River Valley than in any other place in the U.S.A.

Idaho
Gem State

43rd state • Statehood: July 3, 1890 • Population: 1,393,262 • Area: 83,574 square miles

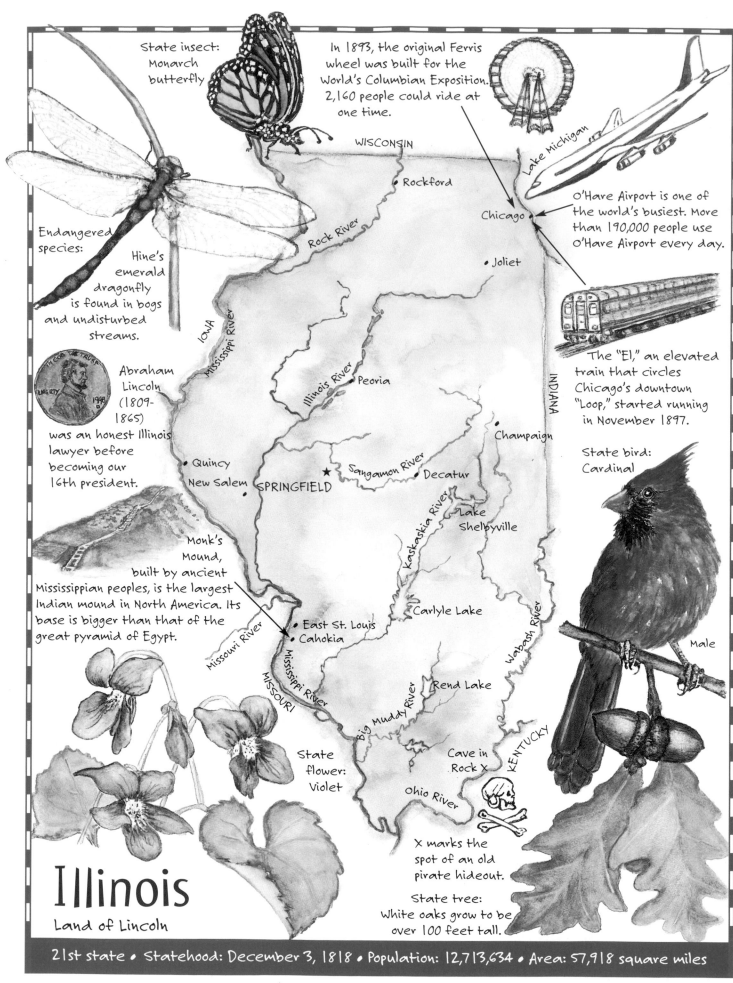

State insect: Monarch butterfly

In 1893, the original Ferris wheel was built for the World's Columbian Exposition. 2,160 people could ride at one time.

WISCONSIN

Rockford

Lake Michigan

O'Hare Airport is one of the world's busiest. More than 190,000 people use O'Hare Airport every day.

Chicago

Joliet

Rock River

Endangered species: Hine's emerald dragonfly is found in bogs and undisturbed streams.

IOWA

Mississippi River

Illinois River

Peoria

INDIANA

The "El," an elevated train that circles Chicago's downtown "Loop," started running in November 1897.

Abraham Lincoln (1809-1865) was an honest Illinois lawyer before becoming our 16th president.

Champaign

State bird: Cardinal

Quincy

New Salem

SPRINGFIELD

Sangamon River

Decatur

Kaskaskia River

Lake Shelbyville

Monk's Mound, built by ancient Mississippian peoples, is the largest Indian mound in North America. Its base is bigger than that of the great pyramid of Egypt.

Carlyle Lake

Male

East St. Louis

Cahokia

Missouri River

Mississippi River

MISSOURI

Big Muddy River

Rend Lake

Wabash River

KENTUCKY

State flower: Violet

Cave in Rock X

Ohio River

X marks the spot of an old pirate hideout.

State tree: White oaks grow to be over 100 feet tall.

Illinois
Land of Lincoln

21st state • Statehood: December 3, 1818 • Population: 12,713,634 • Area: 57,918 square miles

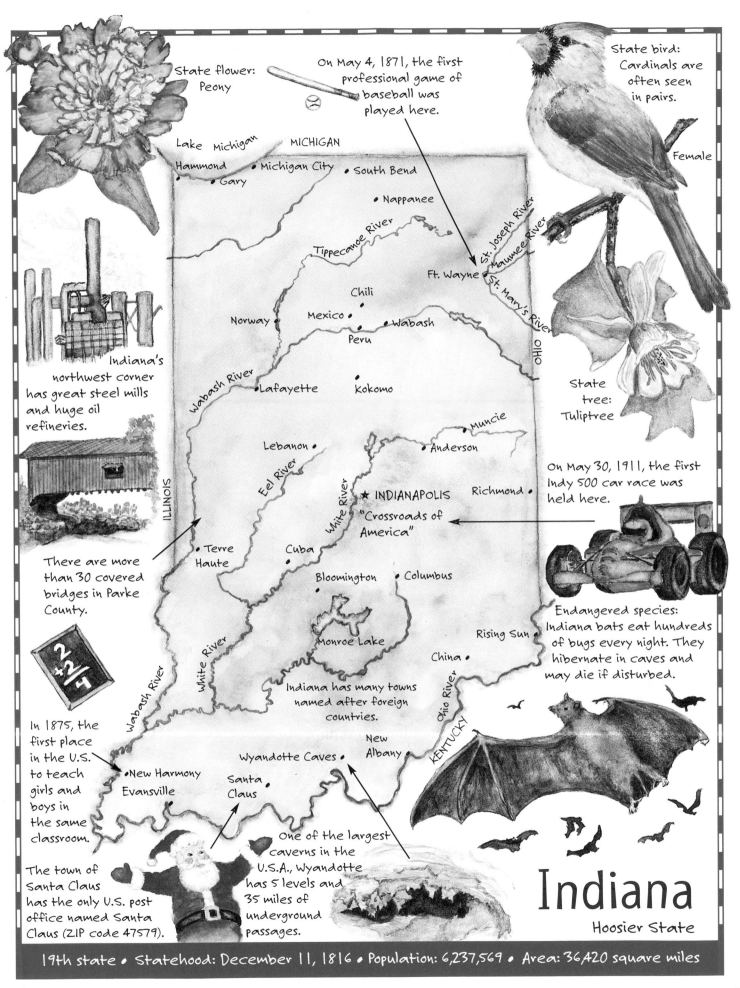

State flower: Peony

On May 4, 1871, the first professional game of baseball was played here.

State bird: Cardinals are often seen in pairs.

Female

MICHIGAN

Lake Michigan

Hammond
• Michigan City   • South Bend
• Gary
    • Nappanee

Tippecanoe River

St. Joseph River
Maumee River
Ft. Wayne
St. Mary's River

OHIO

Chili

Norway   Mexico •   • Wabash
    • Peru

State tree: Tuliptree

Indiana's northwest corner has great steel mills and huge oil refineries.

Wabash River
• Lafayette   Kokomo

    Muncie •
Lebanon •   • Anderson

On May 30, 1911, the first Indy 500 car race was held here.

ILLINOIS

Eel River

White River

★ INDIANAPOLIS
"Crossroads of America"

Richmond •

There are more than 30 covered bridges in Parke County.

2 + 2 / 4

• Terre Haute   • Cuba

• Bloomington   • Columbus

Monroe Lake

Rising Sun •

China •

Endangered species: Indiana bats eat hundreds of bugs every night. They hibernate in caves and may die if disturbed.

White River

Indiana has many towns named after foreign countries.

Ohio River

Wabash River

KENTUCKY

In 1875, the first place in the U.S. to teach girls and boys in the same classroom.

New Albany •

Wyandotte Caves •

• New Harmony
Evansville   Santa Claus

The town of Santa Claus has the only U.S. post office named Santa Claus (ZIP code 47579).

One of the largest caverns in the U.S.A., Wyandotte has 5 levels and 35 miles of underground passages.

Indiana
Hoosier State

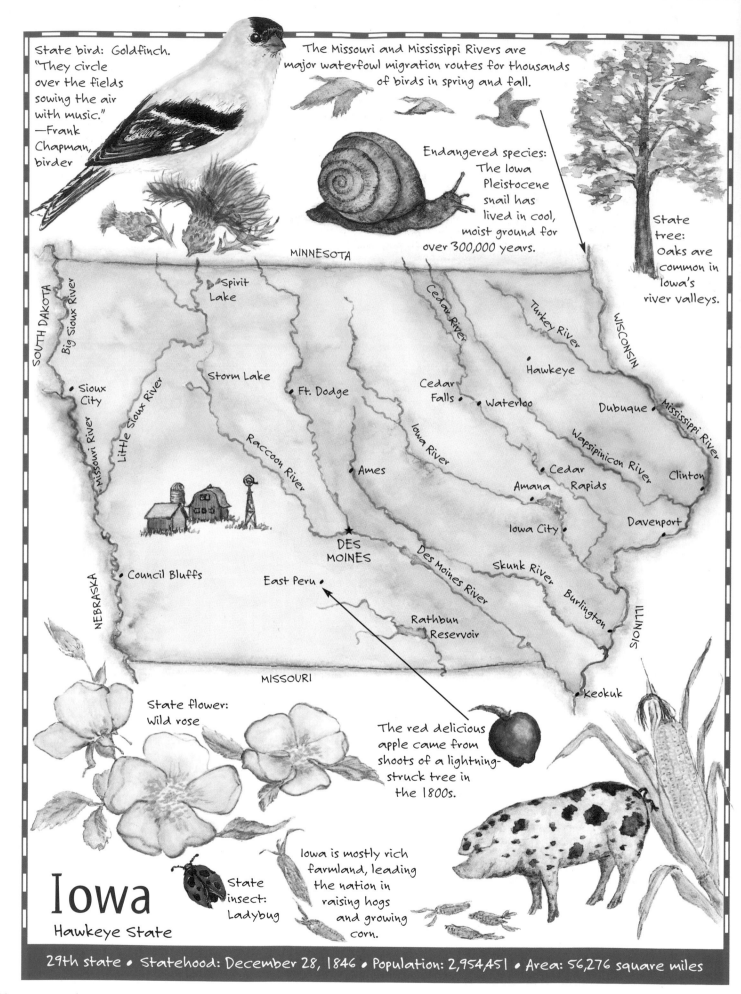

State bird: Goldfinch. "They circle over the fields sowing the air with music." —Frank Chapman, birder

The Missouri and Mississippi Rivers are major waterfowl migration routes for thousands of birds in spring and fall.

Endangered species: The Iowa Pleistocene snail has lived in cool, moist ground for over 300,000 years.

State tree: Oaks are common in Iowa's river valleys.

MINNESOTA

SOUTH DAKOTA

Big Sioux River

Spirit Lake

Cedar River

Turkey River

WISCONSIN

Sioux City

Little Sioux River

Storm Lake

Ft. Dodge

Cedar Falls

Hawkeye

Waterloo

Dubuque

Mississippi River

Missouri River

Raccoon River

Iowa River

Wapsipinicon River

Clinton

Ames

Amana

Cedar Rapids

DES MOINES

Iowa City

Davenport

Council Bluffs

East Peru

Des Moines River

Skunk River

Burlington

ILLINOIS

Rathbun Reservoir

NEBRASKA

MISSOURI

Keokuk

State flower: Wild rose

The red delicious apple came from shoots of a lightning-struck tree in the 1800s.

Iowa
Hawkeye State

State insect: Ladybug

Iowa is mostly rich farmland, leading the nation in raising hogs and growing corn.

29th state • Statehood: December 28, 1846 • Population: 2,954,451 • Area: 56,276 square miles

20

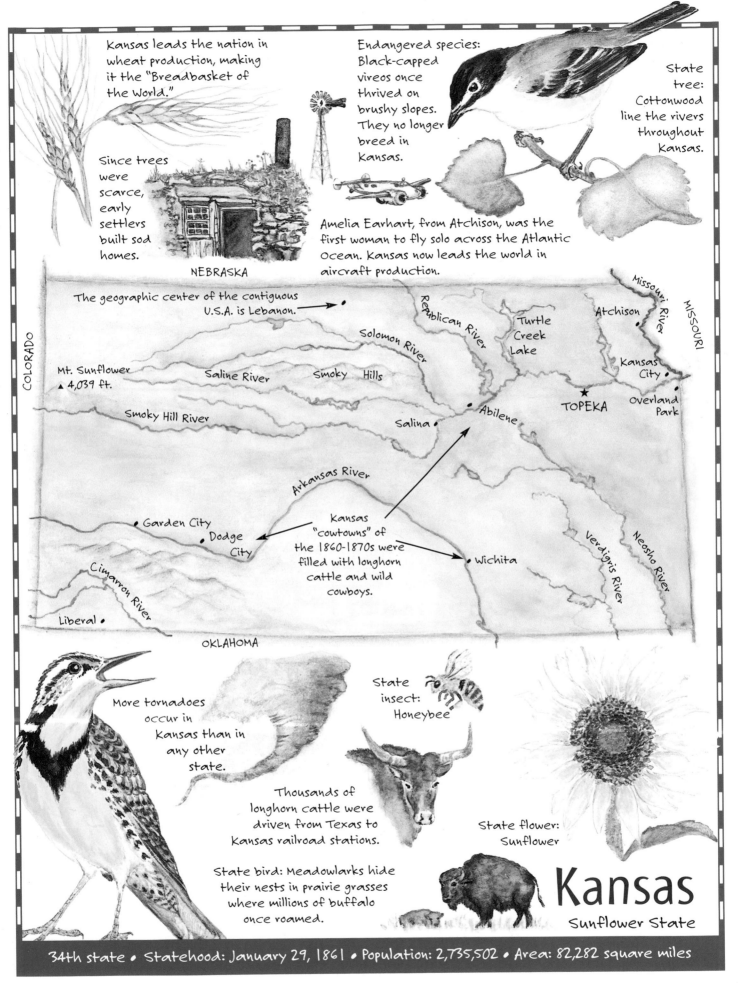

Kansas leads the nation in wheat production, making it the "Breadbasket of the World."

Since trees were scarce, early settlers built sod homes.

NEBRASKA

Endangered species: Black-capped vireos once thrived on brushy slopes. They no longer breed in Kansas.

Amelia Earhart, from Atchison, was the first woman to fly solo across the Atlantic Ocean. Kansas now leads the world in aircraft production.

State tree: Cottonwood line the rivers throughout Kansas.

COLORADO

The geographic center of the contiguous U.S.A. is Lebanon.

Solomon River

Republican River

Turtle Creek Lake

Missouri River

Atchison

MISSOURI

Mt. Sunflower ▲ 4,039 ft.

Saline River

Smoky Hills

Kansas City

Smoky Hill River

Salina

Abilene

TOPEKA

Overland Park

Arkansas River

Garden City

Dodge City

Kansas "cowtowns" of the 1860-1870s were filled with longhorn cattle and wild cowboys.

Wichita

Verdigris River

Neosho River

Cimarron River

Liberal

OKLAHOMA

More tornadoes occur in Kansas than in any other state.

State insect: Honeybee

State flower: Sunflower

Thousands of longhorn cattle were driven from Texas to Kansas railroad stations.

State bird: Meadowlarks hide their nests in prairie grasses where millions of buffalo once roamed.

Kansas
Sunflower State

34th state • Statehood: January 29, 1861 • Population: 2,735,502 • Area: 82,282 square miles

Nutritious bluegrass near Lexington makes it the "Thoroughbred Capital of the World."

State bird: Kentucky cardinal

State tree: Tulip-poplar

In 1938, Bill Monroe and the Blue Grass Boys gave America a unique gift: bluegrass music.

Since 1875 the Kentucky Derby, a world-famous horse race, has been held each May at Churchill Downs.

Ft. Knox guards more gold than any other place in the world. No visitors!

OHIO
Covington
Ohio River
INDIANA
• Louisville
Salt River
▲ Fort Knox
• Owensboro
Rough River
ILLINOIS
Lake Barkley
Paducah •
Kentucky Lake
MISSOURI
Mississippi River
Green River
Birthplace of Jefferson Davis (1808-1889), ▲ president of the Confederacy during the Civil War.
▲ Mammoth Cave
★ FRANKFORT
• Lexington
▲ Birthplace of Abraham Lincoln (1809-1865), president of the Union during the Civil War.
Kentucky River
Cumberland River
Lake Cumberland
Appalachian Mountains
Black Mountain 4,145 ft.
VIRGINIA
WEST VIRGINIA
Big Sandy River Tug Fork
• Ashland
▲ Cumberland Gap
TENNESSEE

The Mammoth Cave system has 340 miles of underground passages. Over 200 animal species are found there.

Endangered species: Kentucky cave shrimp

swim in deep pools of the Mammoth Caves. Their small population is threatened by polluted groundwater.

Kentucky
Bluegrass State

State flower: Goldenrod graces the entire state with a golden glow.

Daniel Boone (1734-1820) led the first white settlers through the dangerous Cumberland Gap into Kentucky in 1775.

15th state • Statehood: June 1, 1792 • Population: 4,145,922 • Area: 40,411 square miles

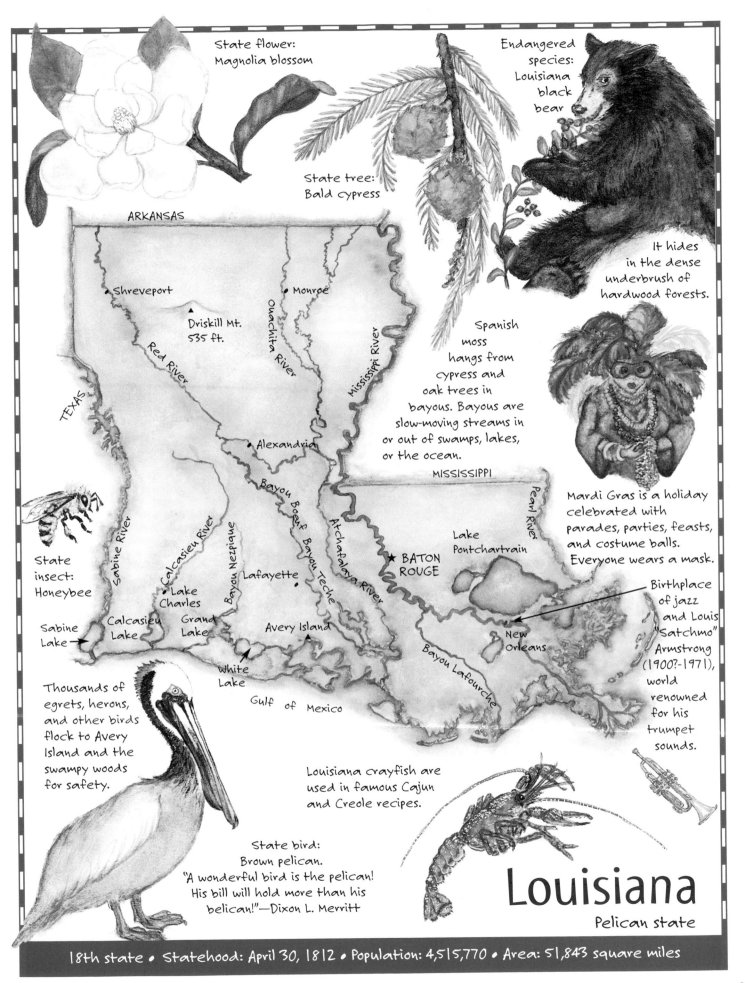

State flower:
Magnolia blossom

Endangered species: Louisiana black bear

State tree:
Bald cypress

It hides in the dense underbrush of hardwood forests.

ARKANSAS

Shreveport

Monroe

Driskill Mt. 535 ft.

Ouachita River

Red River

Mississippi River

TEXAS

Spanish moss hangs from cypress and oak trees in bayous. Bayous are slow-moving streams in or out of swamps, lakes, or the ocean.

Alexandria

MISSISSIPPI

Bayou Boeuf

Bayou Teche

Atchafalaya River

Pearl River

Mardi Gras is a holiday celebrated with parades, parties, feasts, and costume balls. Everyone wears a mask.

Sabine River

Calcasieu River

Bayou Nezpique

Lafayette

Lake Pontchartrain

★ BATON ROUGE

State insect: Honeybee

Lake Charles

Grand Lake

Avery Island

New Orleans

Birthplace of jazz and Louis "Satchmo" Armstrong (1900?-1971), world renowned for his trumpet sounds.

Sabine Lake

Calcasieu Lake

White Lake

Bayou Lafourche

Thousands of egrets, herons, and other birds flock to Avery Island and the swampy woods for safety.

Gulf of Mexico

Louisiana crayfish are used in famous Cajun and Creole recipes.

State bird:
Brown pelican.
"A wonderful bird is the pelican!
His bill will hold more than his
belican!"—Dixon L. Merritt

Louisiana
Pelican state

18th state • Statehood: April 30, 1812 • Population: 4,515,770 • Area: 51,843 square miles

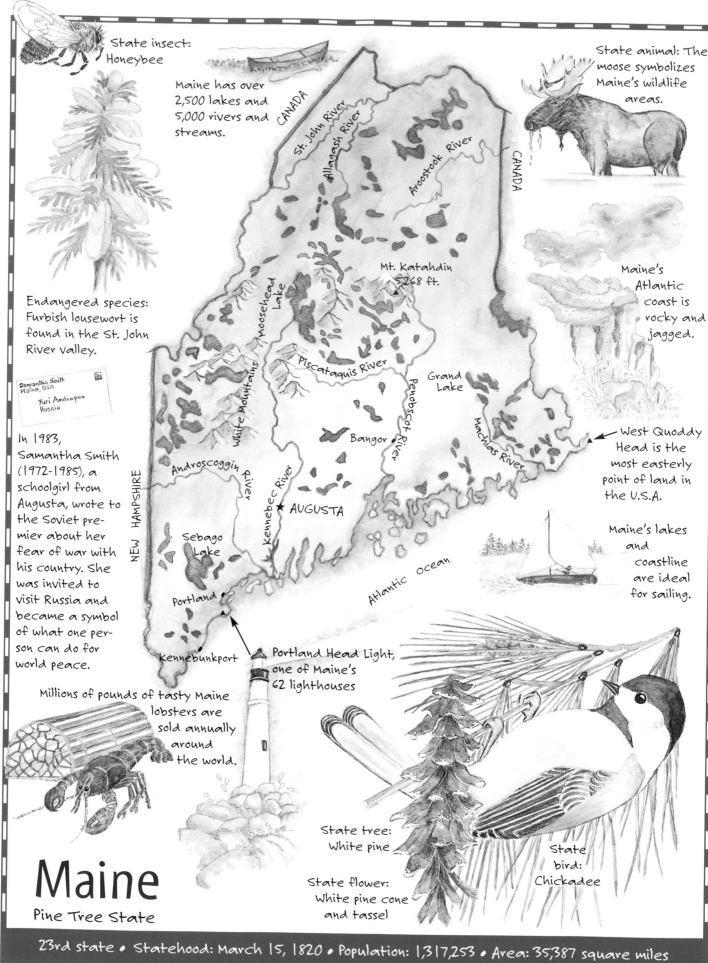

State insect: Honeybee

Maine has over 2,500 lakes and 5,000 rivers and streams.

State animal: The moose symbolizes Maine's wildlife areas.

CANADA

St. John River

Allagash River

Aroostook River

CANADA

Maine's Atlantic coast is rocky and jagged.

Endangered species: Furbish lousewort is found in the St. John River valley.

Mt. Katahdin 5,268 ft.

Moosehead Lake

Piscataquis River

Grand Lake

White Mountains

Penobscot River

Machias River

West Quoddy Head is the most easterly point of land in the U.S.A.

Samantha Smith
Maine, USA

Yuri Andropov
Russia

Bangor

In 1983, Samantha Smith (1972-1985), a schoolgirl from Augusta, wrote to the Soviet premier about her fear of war with his country. She was invited to visit Russia and became a symbol of what one person can do for world peace.

Androscoggin River

Kennebec River

AUGUSTA

NEW HAMPSHIRE

Sebago Lake

Maine's lakes and coastline are ideal for sailing.

Atlantic Ocean

Portland

Kennebunkport

Millions of pounds of tasty Maine lobsters are sold annually around the world.

Portland Head Light, one of Maine's 62 lighthouses

State tree: White pine

State flower: White pine cone and tassel

State bird: Chickadee

Maine
Pine Tree State

23rd state • Statehood: March 15, 1820 • Population: 1,317,253 • Area: 35,387 square miles

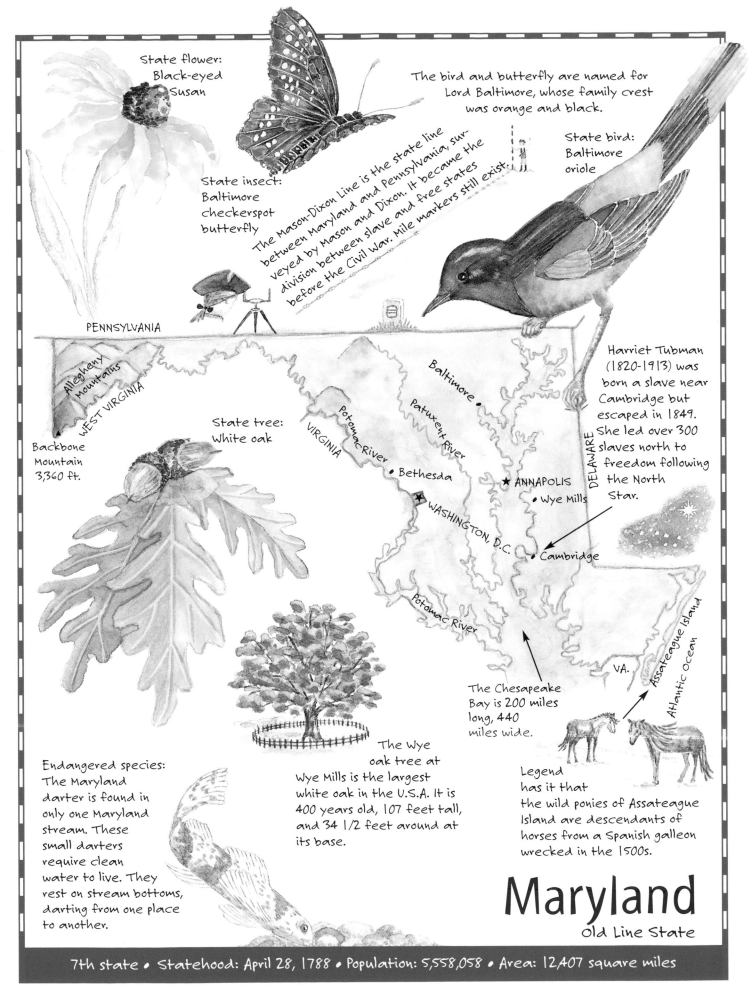

State flower: Black-eyed Susan

State insect: Baltimore checkerspot butterfly

The bird and butterfly are named for Lord Baltimore, whose family crest was orange and black.

State bird: Baltimore oriole

The Mason-Dixon Line is the state line between Maryland and Pennsylvania, surveyed by Mason and Dixon. It became the division between slave and free states before the Civil War. Mile markers still exist.

PENNSYLVANIA

Allegheny Mountains

WEST VIRGINIA

Backbone Mountain 3,360 ft.

State tree: White oak

VIRGINIA

Potomac River

Patuxent River

Baltimore

Bethesda

WASHINGTON, D.C.

★ ANNAPOLIS

Wye Mills

DELAWARE

Harriet Tubman (1820-1913) was born a slave near Cambridge but escaped in 1849. She led over 300 slaves north to freedom following the North Star.

Cambridge

Potomac River

The Chesapeake Bay is 200 miles long, 440 miles wide.

VA.

Assateague Island

Atlantic Ocean

The Wye oak tree at Wye Mills is the largest white oak in the U.S.A. It is 400 years old, 107 feet tall, and 34 1/2 feet around at its base.

Endangered species: The Maryland darter is found in only one Maryland stream. These small darters require clean water to live. They rest on stream bottoms, darting from one place to another.

Legend has it that the wild ponies of Assateague Island are descendants of horses from a Spanish galleon wrecked in the 1500s.

Maryland
Old Line State

7th state • Statehood: April 28, 1788 • Population: 5,558,058 • Area: 12,407 square miles

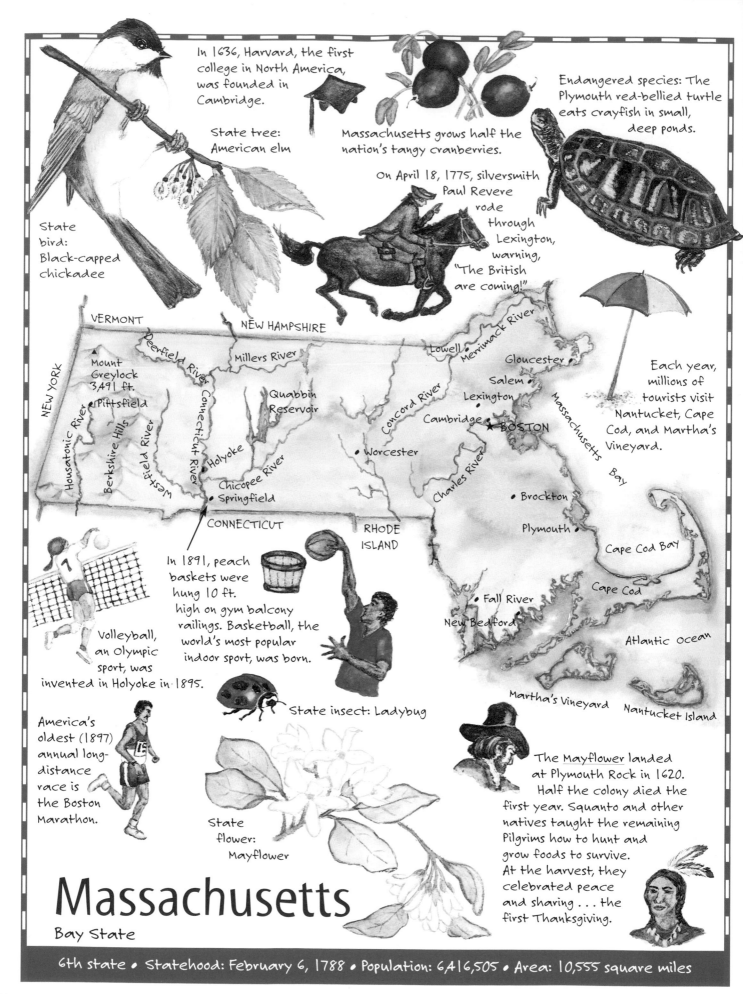

In 1636, Harvard, the first college in North America, was founded in Cambridge.

State tree: American elm

Massachusetts grows half the nation's tangy cranberries.

Endangered species: The Plymouth red-bellied turtle eats crayfish in small, deep ponds.

On April 18, 1775, silversmith Paul Revere rode through Lexington, warning, "The British are coming!"

State bird: Black-capped chickadee

VERMONT
NEW HAMPSHIRE
NEW YORK
Mount Greylock 3,491 ft.
Deerfield River
Millers River
Pittsfield
Housatonic River
Berkshire Hills
Westfield River
Connecticut River
Quabbin Reservoir
Holyoke
Chicopee River
Springfield
CONNECTICUT
Lowell
Merrimack River
Gloucester
Salem
Lexington
Concord River
Cambridge
★ BOSTON
Worcester
Charles River
Massachusetts Bay
RHODE ISLAND
Brockton
Plymouth
Cape Cod Bay
Fall River
New Bedford
Cape Cod
Atlantic Ocean
Martha's Vineyard
Nantucket Island

Each year, millions of tourists visit Nantucket, Cape Cod, and Martha's Vineyard.

In 1891, peach baskets were hung 10 ft. high on gym balcony railings. Basketball, the world's most popular indoor sport, was born.

Volleyball, an Olympic sport, was invented in Holyoke in 1895.

State insect: Ladybug

America's oldest (1897) annual long-distance race is the Boston Marathon.

State flower: Mayflower

The Mayflower landed at Plymouth Rock in 1620. Half the colony died the first year. Squanto and other natives taught the remaining Pilgrims how to hunt and grow foods to survive. At the harvest, they celebrated peace and sharing . . . the first Thanksgiving.

Massachusetts
Bay State

6th state • Statehood: February 6, 1788 • Population: 6,416,505 • Area: 10,555 square miles

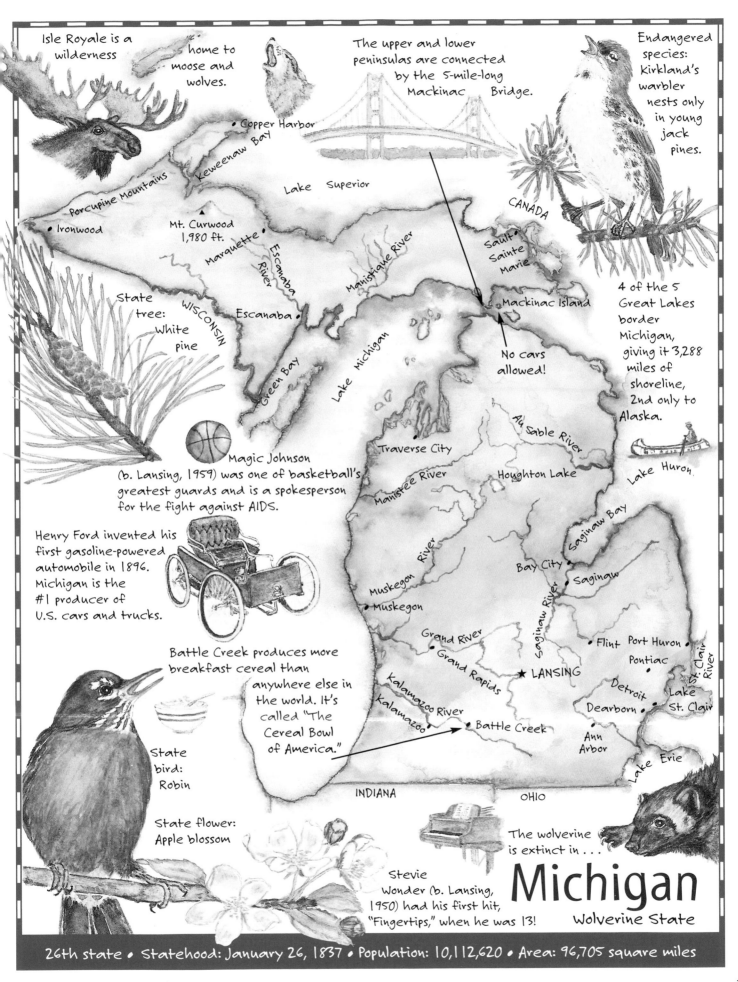

Isle Royale is a wilderness home to moose and wolves.

The upper and lower peninsulas are connected by the 5-mile-long Mackinac Bridge.

Endangered species: Kirkland's warbler nests only in young jack pines.

Copper Harbor

Keweenaw Bay

Lake Superior

CANADA

Porcupine Mountains

Ironwood

Mt. Curwood 1,980 ft.

Marquette

Escanaba River

Manistique River

Sault Sainte Marie

Mackinac Island

No cars allowed!

WISCONSIN

Escanaba

State tree: White pine

Green Bay

Lake Michigan

4 of the 5 Great Lakes border Michigan, giving it 3,288 miles of shoreline, 2nd only to Alaska.

Traverse City

Au Sable River

Houghton Lake

Lake Huron

Magic Johnson (b. Lansing, 1959) was one of basketball's greatest guards and is a spokesperson for the fight against AIDS.

Manistee River

Saginaw Bay

Henry Ford invented his first gasoline-powered automobile in 1896. Michigan is the #1 producer of U.S. cars and trucks.

Muskegon River

Bay City

Saginaw

Saginaw River

Muskegon

Battle Creek produces more breakfast cereal than anywhere else in the world. It's called "The Cereal Bowl of America."

Grand River

Grand Rapids

★ LANSING

Flint

Port Huron

Pontiac

Detroit

Dearborn

Lake St. Clair

St. Clair River

Kalamazoo River

Kalamazoo

Battle Creek

Ann Arbor

Lake Erie

State bird: Robin

State flower: Apple blossom

INDIANA

OHIO

The wolverine is extinct in . . .

Stevie Wonder (b. Lansing, 1950) had his first hit, "Fingertips," when he was 13!

Michigan
Wolverine State

26th state • Statehood: January 26, 1837 • Population: 10,112,620 • Area: 96,705 square miles

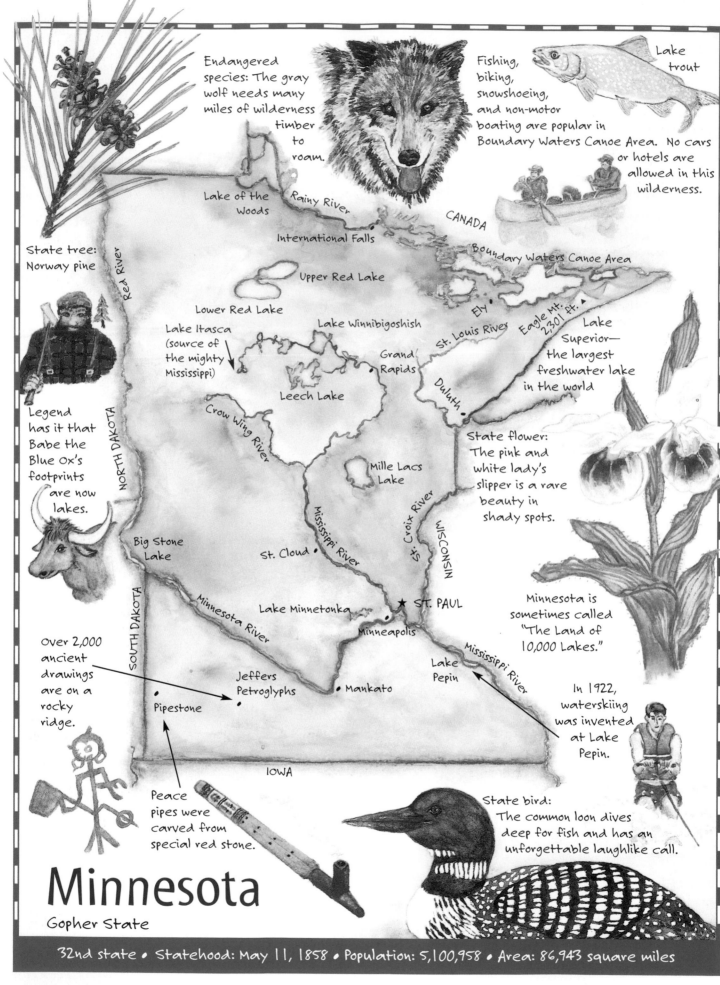

Endangered species: The gray wolf needs many miles of wilderness timber to roam.

Lake trout

Fishing, biking, snowshoeing, and non-motor boating are popular in Boundary Waters Canoe Area. No cars or hotels are allowed in this wilderness.

Lake of the Woods

Rainy River

International Falls

CANADA

Boundary Waters Canoe Area

State tree: Norway pine

Red River

Upper Red Lake

Lower Red Lake

Lake Winnibigoshish

Ely

Eagle Mt. 2,301 ft.

St. Louis River

Lake Superior—the largest freshwater lake in the world

Lake Itasca (source of the mighty Mississippi)

Grand Rapids

Duluth

Legend has it that Babe the Blue Ox's footprints are now lakes.

NORTH DAKOTA

Leech Lake

Crow Wing River

Mille Lacs Lake

State flower: The pink and white lady's slipper is a rare beauty in shady spots.

Big Stone Lake

St. Cloud

Mississippi River

St. Croix River

WISCONSIN

Minnesota is sometimes called "The Land of 10,000 Lakes."

SOUTH DAKOTA

Minnesota River

Lake Minnetonka

★ ST. PAUL

Minneapolis

Mississippi River

Over 2,000 ancient drawings are on a rocky ridge.

Jeffers Petroglyphs

Mankato

Lake Pepin

In 1922, waterskiing was invented at Lake Pepin.

Pipestone

IOWA

Peace pipes were carved from special red stone.

State bird: The common loon dives deep for fish and has an unforgettable laughlike call.

Minnesota
Gopher State

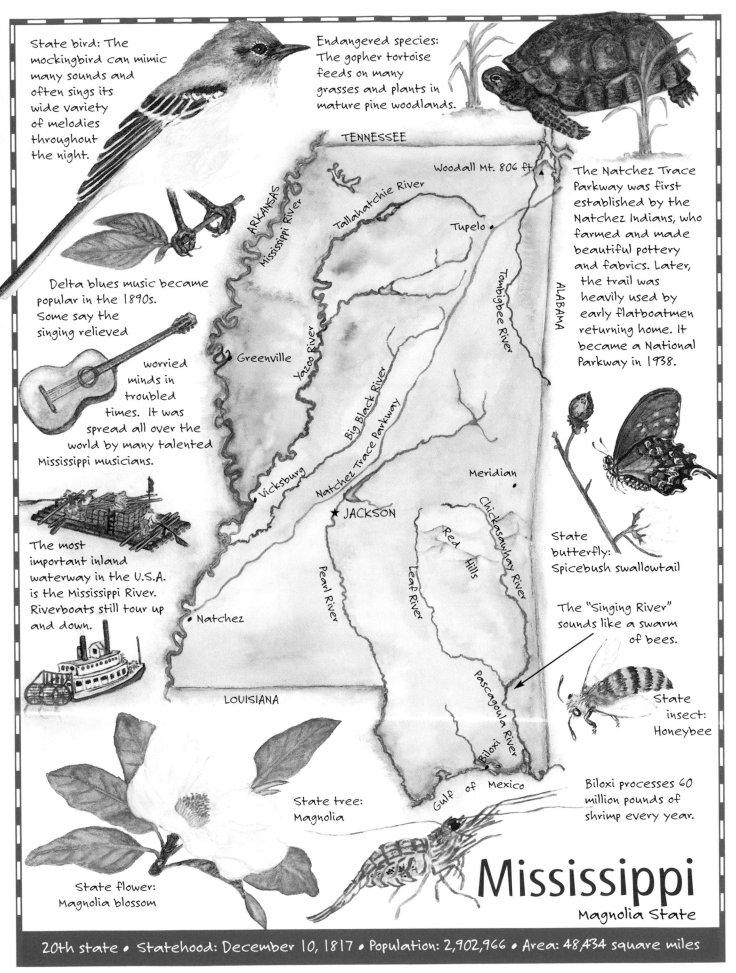

State bird: The mockingbird can mimic many sounds and often sings its wide variety of melodies throughout the night.

Endangered species: The gopher tortoise feeds on many grasses and plants in mature pine woodlands.

Delta blues music became popular in the 1890s. Some say the singing relieved worried minds in troubled times. It was spread all over the world by many talented Mississippi musicians.

The most important inland waterway in the U.S.A. is the Mississippi River. Riverboats still tour up and down.

The Natchez Trace Parkway was first established by the Natchez Indians, who farmed and made beautiful pottery and fabrics. Later, the trail was heavily used by early flatboatmen returning home. It became a National Parkway in 1938.

State butterfly: Spicebush swallowtail

The "Singing River" sounds like a swarm of bees.

State insect: Honeybee

Biloxi processes 60 million pounds of shrimp every year.

State tree: Magnolia

State flower: Magnolia blossom

TENNESSEE

Woodall Mt. 806 ft.

ARKANSAS

Mississippi River

Tallahatchie River

Tupelo

Tombigbee River

ALABAMA

Yazoo River

Greenville

Big Black River

Natchez Trace Parkway

Vicksburg

Meridian

JACKSON

Chickasawhay River

Red Hills

Natchez

Pearl River

Leaf River

Pascagoula River

LOUISIANA

Biloxi

Gulf of Mexico

Mississippi

Magnolia State

20th state • Statehood: December 10, 1817 • Population: 2,902,966 • Area: 48,434 square miles

29

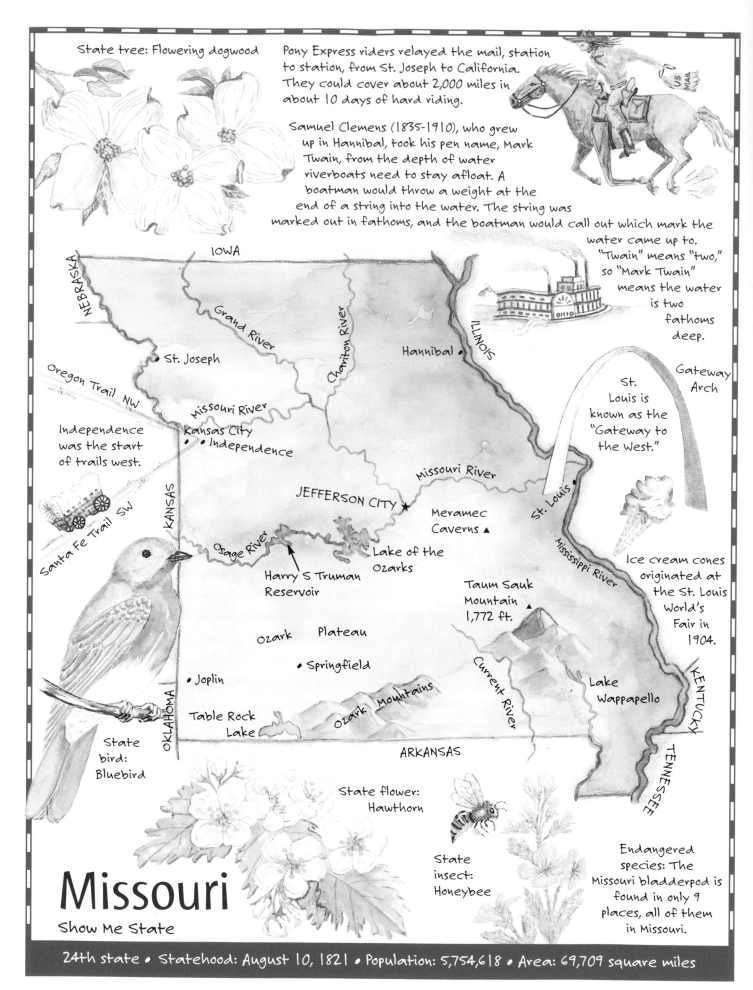

State tree: Flowering dogwood

Pony Express riders relayed the mail, station to station, from St. Joseph to California. They could cover about 2,000 miles in about 10 days of hard riding.

Samuel Clemens (1835-1910), who grew up in Hannibal, took his pen name, Mark Twain, from the depth of water riverboats need to stay afloat. A boatman would throw a weight at the end of a string into the water. The string was marked out in fathoms, and the boatman would call out which mark the water came up to. "Twain" means "two," so "Mark Twain" means the water is two fathoms deep.

St. Louis is known as the "Gateway to the West."

Gateway Arch

Ice cream cones originated at the St. Louis World's Fair in 1904.

IOWA

NEBRASKA

Grand River

Chariton River

ILLINOIS

Hannibal

St. Joseph

Oregon Trail NW

Missouri River

Independence was the start of trails west.

Kansas City

Independence

KANSAS

Santa Fe Trail SW

JEFFERSON CITY

Missouri River

St. Louis

Meramec Caverns ▲

Osage River

Harry S Truman Reservoir

Lake of the Ozarks

Mississippi River

Taum Sauk Mountain 1,772 ft. ▲

Ozark   Plateau

Springfield

Current River

Lake Wappapello

KENTUCKY

Joplin

Table Rock Lake

Ozark Mountains

OKLAHOMA

State bird: Bluebird

ARKANSAS

TENNESSEE

State flower: Hawthorn

State insect: Honeybee

Endangered species: The Missouri bladderpod is found in only 9 places, all of them in Missouri.

Missouri

Show Me State

24th state • Statehood: August 10, 1821 • Population: 5,754,618 • Area: 69,709 square miles

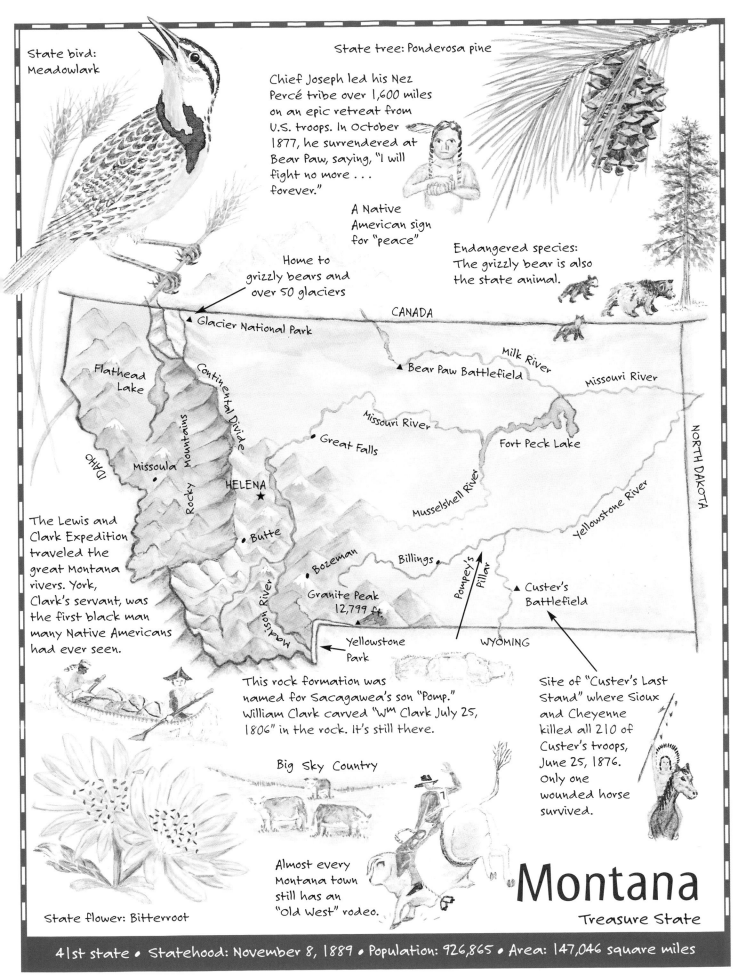

State bird: Meadowlark

State tree: Ponderosa pine

Chief Joseph led his Nez Percé tribe over 1,600 miles on an epic retreat from U.S. troops. In October 1877, he surrendered at Bear Paw, saying, "I will fight no more . . . forever."

A Native American sign for "peace"

Endangered species: The grizzly bear is also the state animal.

Home to grizzly bears and over 50 glaciers

CANADA

Glacier National Park

Flathead Lake

Continental Divide

Milk River

Bear Paw Battlefield

Missouri River

Missouri River

Great Falls

Fort Peck Lake

Rocky Mountains

Missoula

HELENA

Butte

Musselshell River

NORTH DAKOTA

IDAHO

The Lewis and Clark Expedition traveled the great Montana rivers. York, Clark's servant, was the first black man many Native Americans had ever seen.

Bozeman

Billings

Pompey's Pillar

Yellowstone River

Custer's Battlefield

Granite Peak 12,799 ft.

Madison River

Yellowstone Park

WYOMING

This rock formation was named for Sacagawea's son "Pomp." William Clark carved "Wm Clark July 25, 1806" in the rock. It's still there.

Site of "Custer's Last Stand" where Sioux and Cheyenne killed all 210 of Custer's troops, June 25, 1876. Only one wounded horse survived.

Big Sky Country

Almost every Montana town still has an "Old West" rodeo.

State flower: Bitterroot

Montana
Treasure State

41st state • Statehood: November 8, 1889 • Population: 926,865 • Area: 147,046 square miles

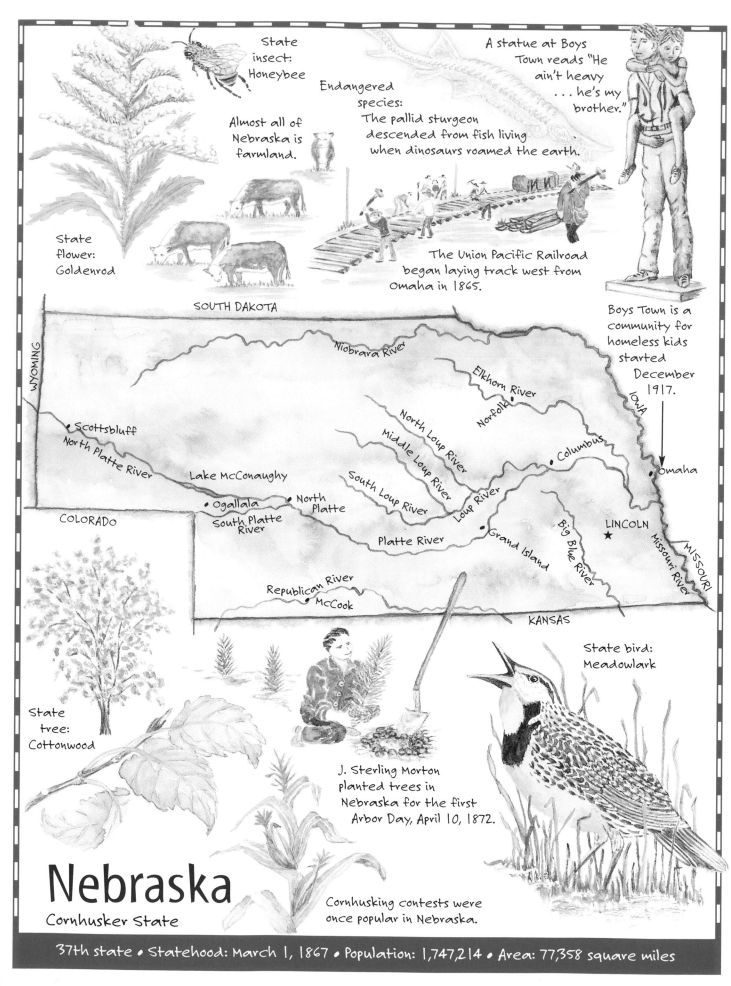

State insect: Honeybee

Endangered species: The pallid sturgeon descended from fish living when dinosaurs roamed the earth.

A statue at Boys Town reads "He ain't heavy . . . he's my brother."

Almost all of Nebraska is farmland.

State flower: Goldenrod

The Union Pacific Railroad began laying track west from Omaha in 1865.

Boys Town is a community for homeless kids started December 1917.

SOUTH DAKOTA

WYOMING

Niobrara River

Elkhorn River

Norfolk

North Loup River

Middle Loup River

Scottsbluff

North Platte River

Columbus

IOWA

Lake McConaughy

South Loup River

Loup River

Omaha

Ogallala

North Platte

COLORADO

South Platte River

Big Blue River

LINCOLN

Platte River

Grand Island

Missouri River

MISSOURI

Republican River

McCook

KANSAS

State tree: Cottonwood

J. Sterling Morton planted trees in Nebraska for the first Arbor Day, April 10, 1872.

State bird: Meadowlark

Nebraska
Cornhusker State

Cornhusking contests were once popular in Nebraska.

37th state • Statehood: March 1, 1867 • Population: 1,747,214 • Area: 77,358 square miles

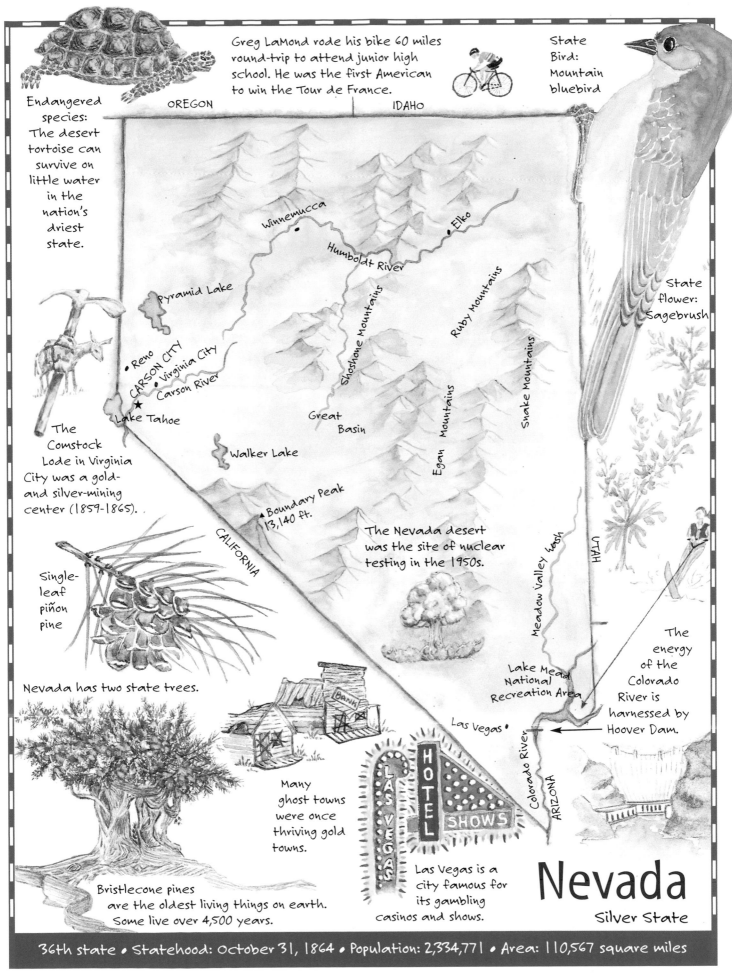

Endangered species: The desert tortoise can survive on little water in the nation's driest state.

Greg LaMond rode his bike 60 miles round-trip to attend junior high school. He was the first American to win the Tour de France.

State Bird: Mountain bluebird

OREGON

IDAHO

Winnemucca

Elko

Humboldt River

Pyramid Lake

Shoshone Mountains

Ruby Mountains

State flower: Sagebrush

Reno
CARSON CITY
Virginia City
Carson River

Lake Tahoe

Great Basin

Egan Mountains

Snake Mountains

The Comstock Lode in Virginia City was a gold- and silver-mining center (1859-1865).

Walker Lake

Boundary Peak 13,140 ft.

The Nevada desert was the site of nuclear testing in the 1950s.

CALIFORNIA

Single-leaf piñon pine

UTAH

Meadow Valley Wash

The energy of the Colorado River is harnessed by Hoover Dam.

Lake Mead National Recreation Area

Nevada has two state trees.

Las Vegas

Colorado River

ARIZONA

Many ghost towns were once thriving gold towns.

LAS VEGAS HOTEL SHOWS

Las Vegas is a city famous for its gambling casinos and shows.

Nevada
Silver State

Bristlecone pines are the oldest living things on earth. Some live over 4,500 years.

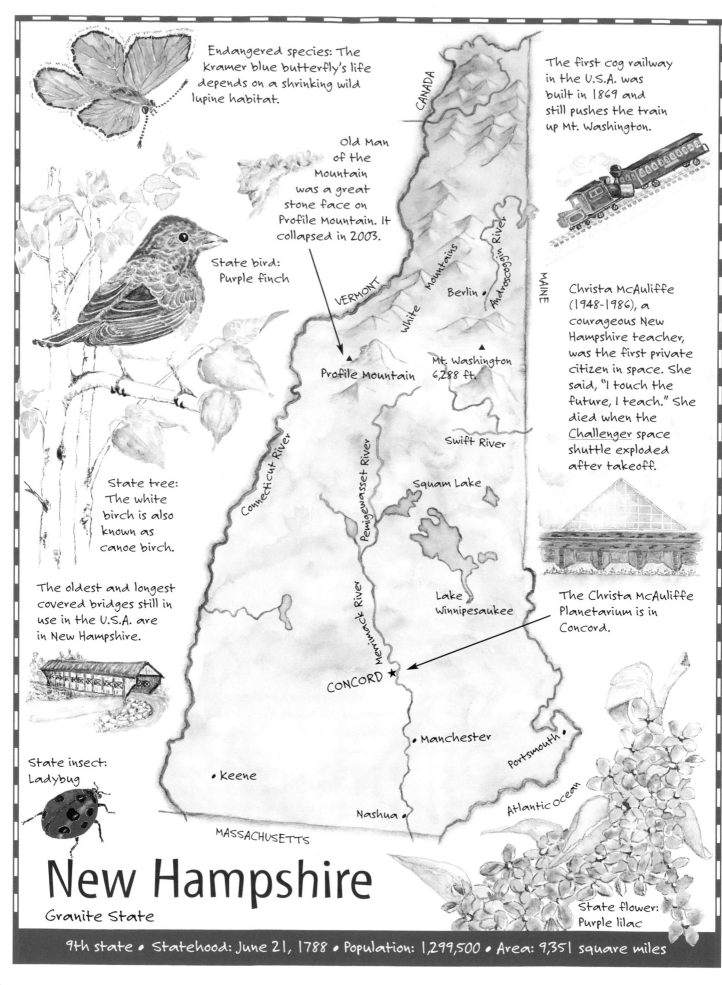

Endangered species: The Kramer blue butterfly's life depends on a shrinking wild lupine habitat.

Old Man of the Mountain was a great stone face on Profile Mountain. It collapsed in 2003.

The first cog railway in the U.S.A. was built in 1869 and still pushes the train up Mt. Washington.

State bird: Purple finch

Christa McAuliffe (1948-1986), a courageous New Hampshire teacher, was the first private citizen in space. She said, "I touch the future, I teach." She died when the Challenger space shuttle exploded after takeoff.

State tree: The white birch is also known as canoe birch.

The oldest and longest covered bridges still in use in the U.S.A. are in New Hampshire.

The Christa McAuliffe Planetarium is in Concord.

State insect: Ladybug

State flower: Purple lilac

CANADA

VERMONT

MAINE

Berlin

Androscoggin River

White Mountains

Profile Mountain

Mt. Washington 6,288 ft.

Swift River

Connecticut River

Pemigewasset River

Squam Lake

Merrimack River

Lake Winnipesaukee

CONCORD ★

Manchester

Portsmouth

Keene

Atlantic Ocean

Nashua

MASSACHUSETTS

New Hampshire
Granite State

9th state • Statehood: June 21, 1788 • Population: 1,299,500 • Area: 9,351 square miles

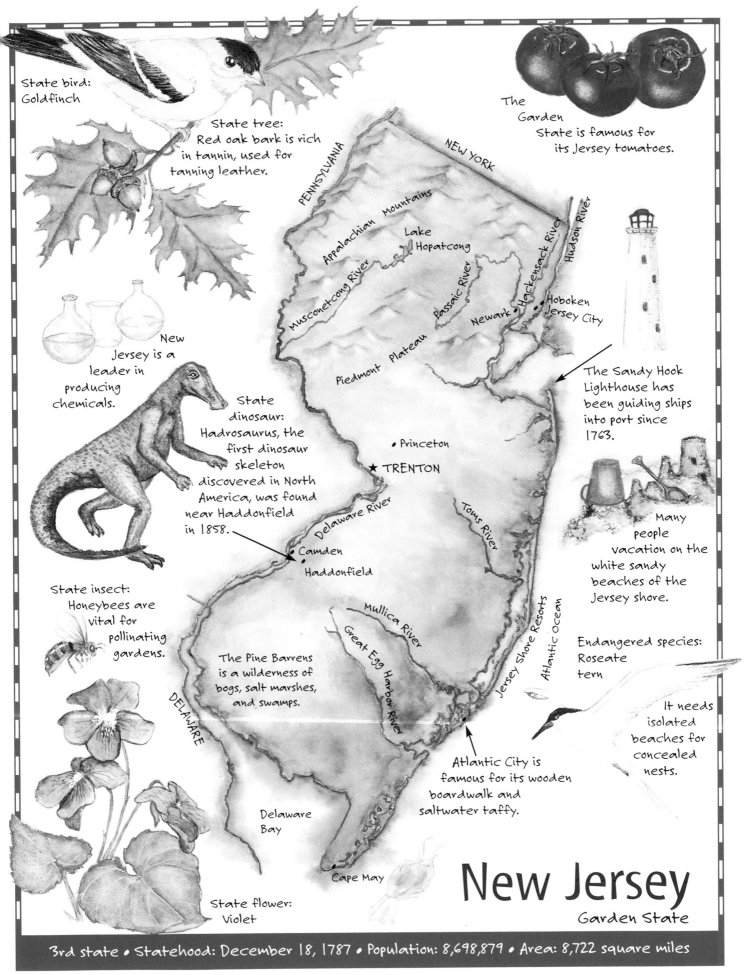

State bird: Goldfinch

State tree: Red oak bark is rich in tannin, used for tanning leather.

The Garden State is famous for its Jersey tomatoes.

New Jersey is a leader in producing chemicals.

State dinosaur: Hadrosaurus, the first dinosaur skeleton discovered in North America, was found near Haddonfield in 1858.

State insect: Honeybees are vital for pollinating gardens.

The Pine Barrens is a wilderness of bogs, salt marshes, and swamps.

The Sandy Hook Lighthouse has been guiding ships into port since 1763.

Many people vacation on the white sandy beaches of the Jersey shore.

Endangered species: Roseate tern

It needs isolated beaches for concealed nests.

Atlantic City is famous for its wooden boardwalk and saltwater taffy.

State flower: Violet

PENNSYLVANIA
NEW YORK
Appalachian Mountains
Lake Hopatcong
Musconetcong River
Passaic River
Hackensack River
Hudson River
Newark • Hoboken
Jersey City
Piedmont Plateau
• Princeton
★ TRENTON
Delaware River
• Camden
Haddonfield
Toms River
Mullica River
Great Egg Harbor River
Jersey Shore Resorts
Atlantic Ocean
DELAWARE
Delaware Bay
Cape May

New Jersey
Garden State

3rd state • Statehood: December 18, 1787 • Population: 8,698,879 • Area: 8,722 square miles

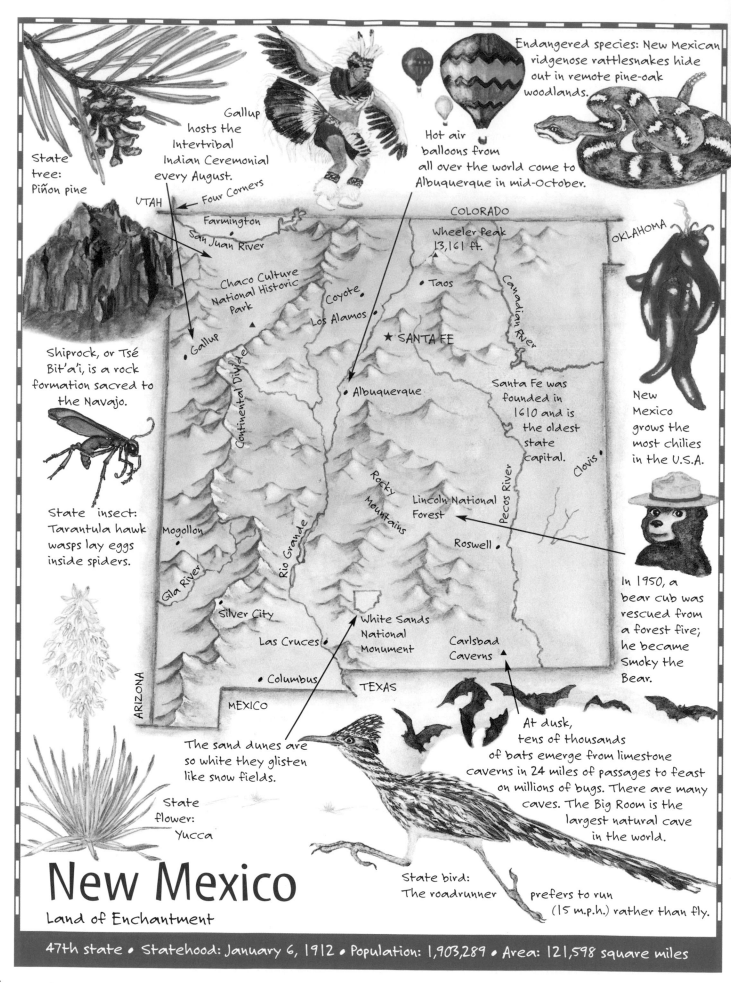

State tree: Piñon pine

Gallup hosts the Intertribal Indian Ceremonial every August.

Hot air balloons from all over the world come to Albuquerque in mid-October.

Endangered species: New Mexican ridgenose rattlesnakes hide out in remote pine-oak woodlands.

Shiprock, or Tsé Bit'a'i, is a rock formation sacred to the Navajo.

State insect: Tarantula hawk wasps lay eggs inside spiders.

New Mexico grows the most chilies in the U.S.A.

In 1950, a bear cub was rescued from a forest fire; he became Smoky the Bear.

Santa Fe was founded in 1610 and is the oldest state capital.

UTAH
Four Corners
Farmington
San Juan River
Chaco Culture National Historic Park
Gallup
Continental Divide
Mogollon
Gila River
Silver City
Las Cruces
Columbus
ARIZONA
MEXICO

COLORADO
Wheeler Peak 13,161 ft.
Taos
Coyote
Los Alamos
★ SANTA FE
Albuquerque
Canadian River
Rocky Mountains
Lincoln National Forest
Pecos River
Roswell
Clovis
White Sands National Monument
Carlsbad Caverns
TEXAS
OKLAHOMA

The sand dunes are so white they glisten like snow fields.

State flower: Yucca

At dusk, tens of thousands of bats emerge from limestone caverns in 24 miles of passages to feast on millions of bugs. There are many caves. The Big Room is the largest natural cave in the world.

New Mexico
Land of Enchantment

State bird: The roadrunner prefers to run (15 m.p.h.) rather than fly.

47th state • Statehood: January 6, 1912 • Population: 1,903,289 • Area: 121,598 square miles

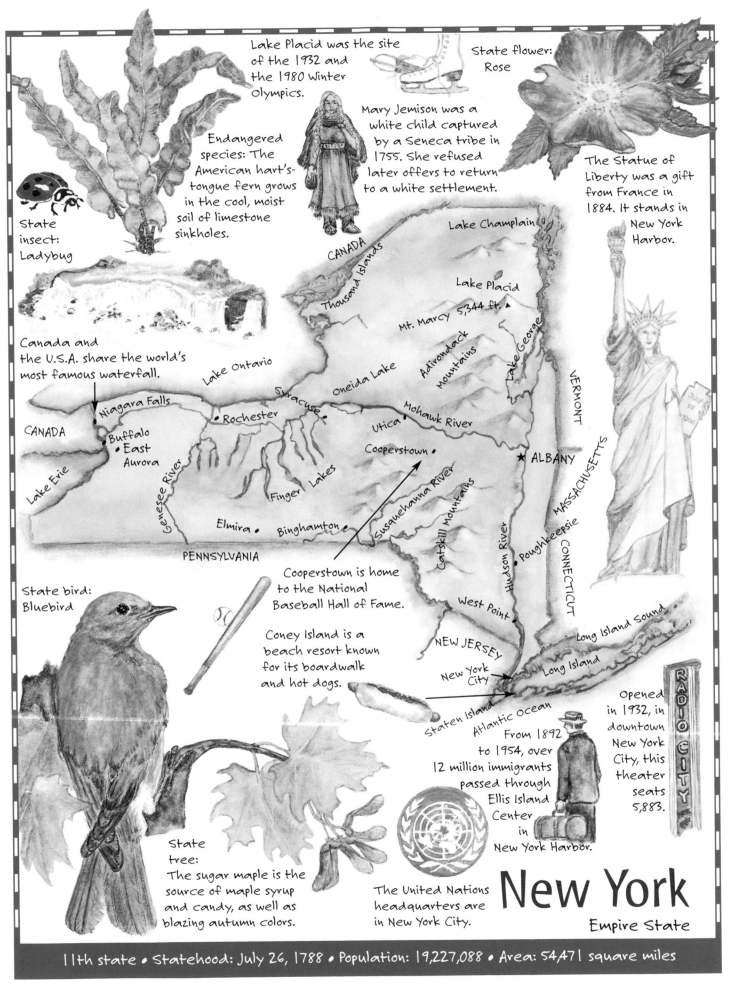

Lake Placid was the site of the 1932 and the 1980 Winter Olympics.

State flower: Rose

Mary Jemison was a white child captured by a Seneca tribe in 1755. She refused later offers to return to a white settlement.

Endangered species: The American hart's-tongue fern grows in the cool, moist soil of limestone sinkholes.

The Statue of Liberty was a gift from France in 1884. It stands in New York Harbor.

State insect: Ladybug

Canada and the U.S.A. share the world's most famous waterfall.

CANADA

Lake Champlain

Thousand Islands

Lake Placid

Mt. Marcy 5,344 ft.

Adirondack Mountains

Lake George

VERMONT

Lake Ontario

Syracuse

Oneida Lake

Mohawk River

Niagara Falls

Rochester

Utica

Cooperstown

ALBANY

MASSACHUSETTS

CANADA

Buffalo
East Aurora

Genesee River

Finger Lakes

Susquehanna River

Catskill Mountains

Hudson River

Poughkeepsie

CONNECTICUT

Lake Erie

Elmira

Binghamton

PENNSYLVANIA

Cooperstown is home to the National Baseball Hall of Fame.

West Point

Long Island Sound

Coney Island is a beach resort known for its boardwalk and hot dogs.

NEW JERSEY

New York City

Long Island

RADIO CITY

State bird: Bluebird

Staten Island

Atlantic Ocean

From 1892 to 1954, over 12 million immigrants passed through Ellis Island Center in New York Harbor.

Opened in 1932, in downtown New York City, this theater seats 5,883.

State tree: The sugar maple is the source of maple syrup and candy, as well as blazing autumn colors.

The United Nations headquarters are in New York City.

New York

Empire State

11th state • Statehood: July 26, 1788 • Population: 19,227,088 • Area: 54,471 square miles

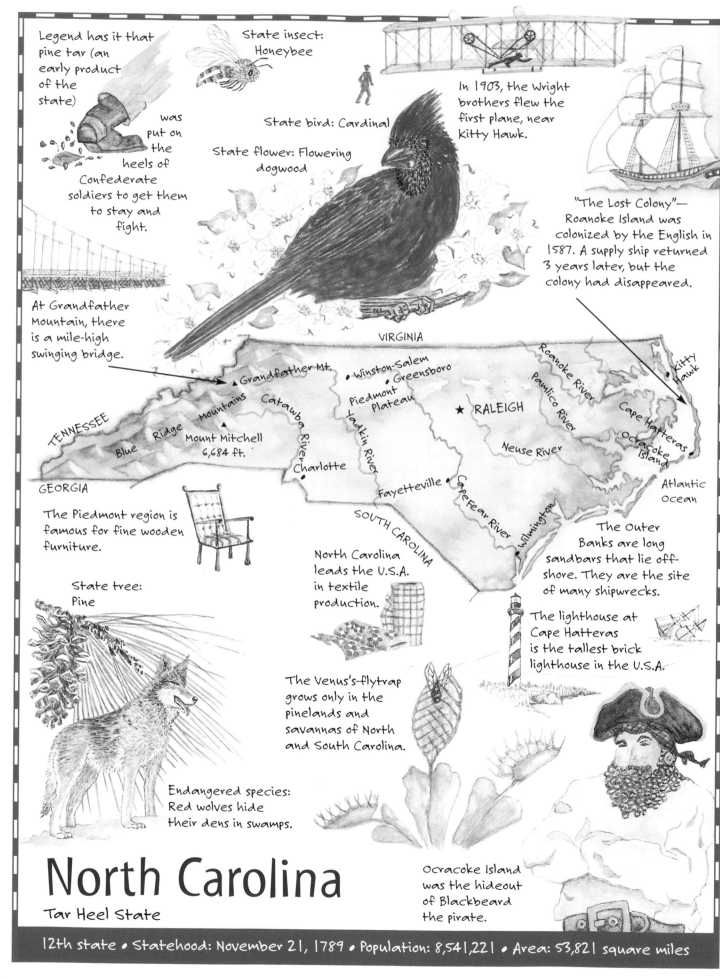

Legend has it that pine tar (an early product of the state) was put on the heels of Confederate soldiers to get them to stay and fight.

State insect: Honeybee

In 1903, the Wright brothers flew the first plane, near Kitty Hawk.

State bird: Cardinal

State flower: Flowering dogwood

"The Lost Colony"— Roanoke Island was colonized by the English in 1587. A supply ship returned 3 years later, but the colony had disappeared.

At Grandfather Mountain, there is a mile-high swinging bridge.

VIRGINIA

Grandfather Mt.
Winston-Salem • Greensboro
Piedmont Plateau
Roanoke River
Kitty Hawk

TENNESSEE

Blue Ridge Mountains
Catawba River
Yadkin River
★ RALEIGH
Pawlico River
Cape Hatteras
Ocracoke Island

Mount Mitchell 6,684 ft.
Neuse River

GEORGIA
Charlotte

Atlantic Ocean

The Piedmont region is famous for fine wooden furniture.

Fayetteville •
Cape Fear River
Wilmington

SOUTH CAROLINA

North Carolina leads the U.S.A. in textile production.

The Outer Banks are long sandbars that lie offshore. They are the site of many shipwrecks.

State tree: Pine

The lighthouse at Cape Hatteras is the tallest brick lighthouse in the U.S.A.

The Venus's-flytrap grows only in the pinelands and savannas of North and South Carolina.

Endangered species: Red wolves hide their dens in swamps.

North Carolina
Tar Heel State

Ocracoke Island was the hideout of Blackbeard the pirate.

12th state • Statehood: November 21, 1789 • Population: 8,541,221 • Area: 53,821 square miles

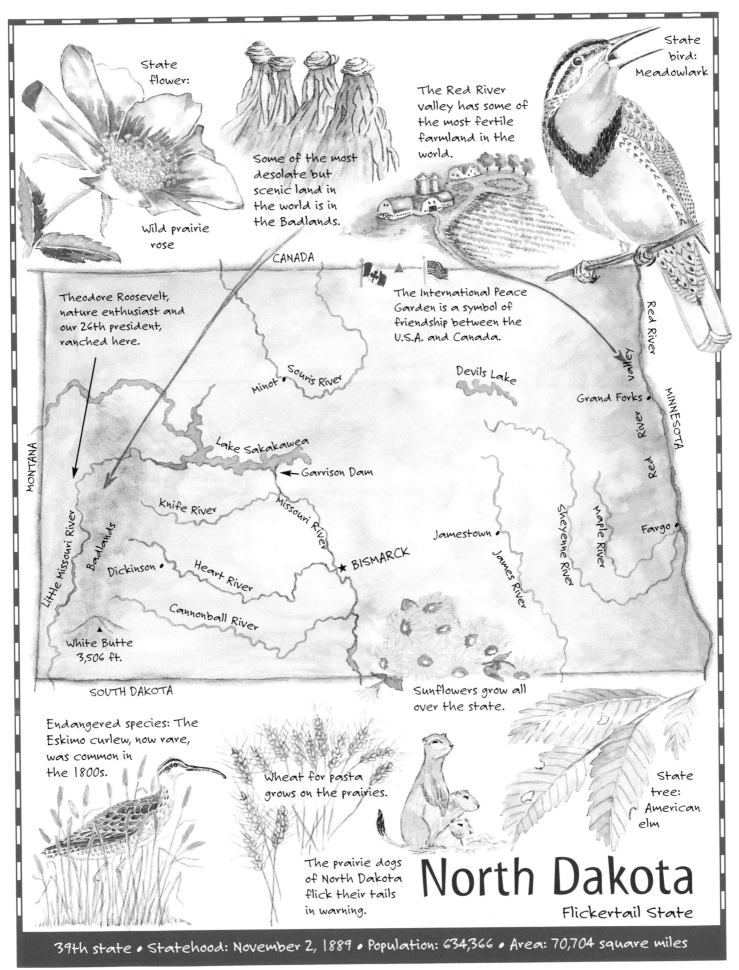

State flower:

Wild prairie rose

Some of the most desolate but scenic land in the world is in the Badlands.

The Red River valley has some of the most fertile farmland in the world.

State bird: Meadowlark

CANADA

Theodore Roosevelt, nature enthusiast and our 26th president, ranched here.

The International Peace Garden is a symbol of friendship between the U.S.A. and Canada.

Red River valley

Minot • Souris River

Devils Lake

Grand Forks •

MINNESOTA

MONTANA

Lake Sakakawea

← Garrison Dam

Knife River

Missouri River

Red River

Maple River

Fargo •

Little Missouri River

Badlands

Dickinson •

Heart River

BISMARCK ★

Jamestown •

Sheyenne River

James River

White Butte 3,506 ft.

Cannonball River

SOUTH DAKOTA

Sunflowers grow all over the state.

Endangered species: The Eskimo curlew, now rare, was common in the 1800s.

Wheat for pasta grows on the prairies.

State tree: American elm

The prairie dogs of North Dakota flick their tails in warning.

North Dakota
Flickertail State

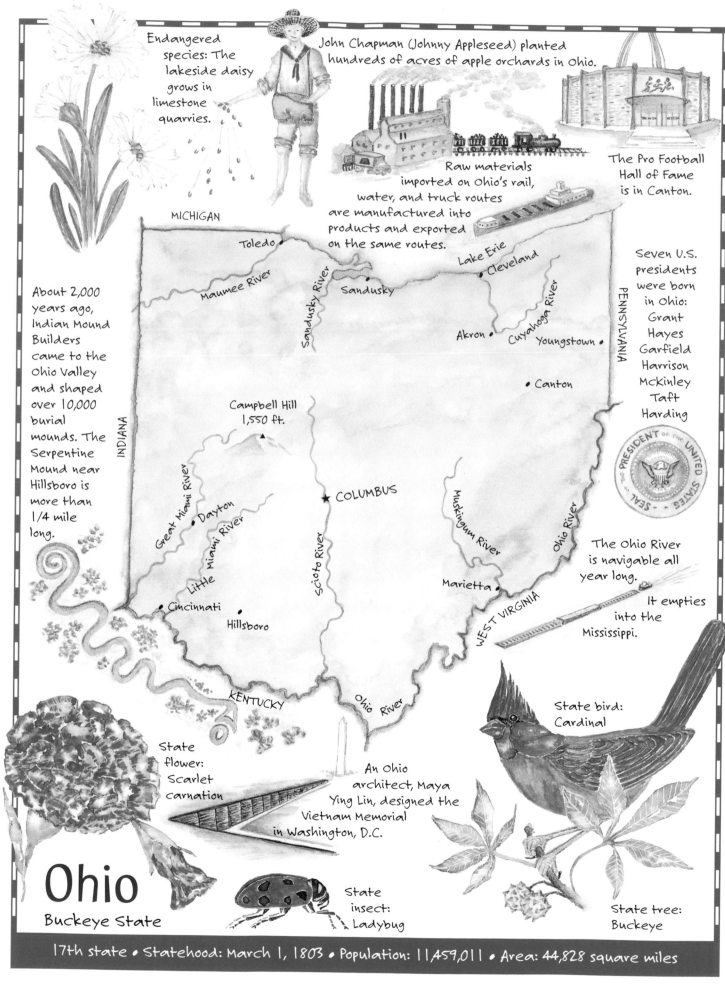

Endangered species: The lakeside daisy grows in limestone quarries.

John Chapman (Johnny Appleseed) planted hundreds of acres of apple orchards in Ohio.

Raw materials imported on Ohio's rail, water, and truck routes are manufactured into products and exported on the same routes.

The Pro Football Hall of Fame is in Canton.

MICHIGAN

Toledo

Maumee River

Sandusky River

Sandusky

Lake Erie

Cleveland

Akron

Cuyahoga River

Youngstown

PENNSYLVANIA

Canton

Seven U.S. presidents were born in Ohio: Grant Hayes Garfield Harrison Mckinley Taft Harding

About 2,000 years ago, Indian Mound Builders came to the Ohio Valley and shaped over 10,000 burial mounds. The Serpentine Mound near Hillsboro is more than 1/4 mile long.

INDIANA

Campbell Hill 1,550 ft.

Great Miami River

Dayton

Miami River

Little

Cincinnati

Hillsboro

★ COLUMBUS

Scioto River

Muskingum River

Ohio River

SEAL OF THE PRESIDENT OF THE UNITED STATES

The Ohio River is navigable all year long.

Marietta

WEST VIRGINIA

It empties into the Mississippi.

KENTUCKY

Ohio River

State bird: Cardinal

State flower: Scarlet carnation

An Ohio architect, Maya Ying Lin, designed the Vietnam Memorial in Washington, D.C.

State insect: Ladybug

State tree: Buckeye

Ohio
Buckeye State

17th state • Statehood: March 1, 1803 • Population: 11,459,011 • Area: 44,828 square miles

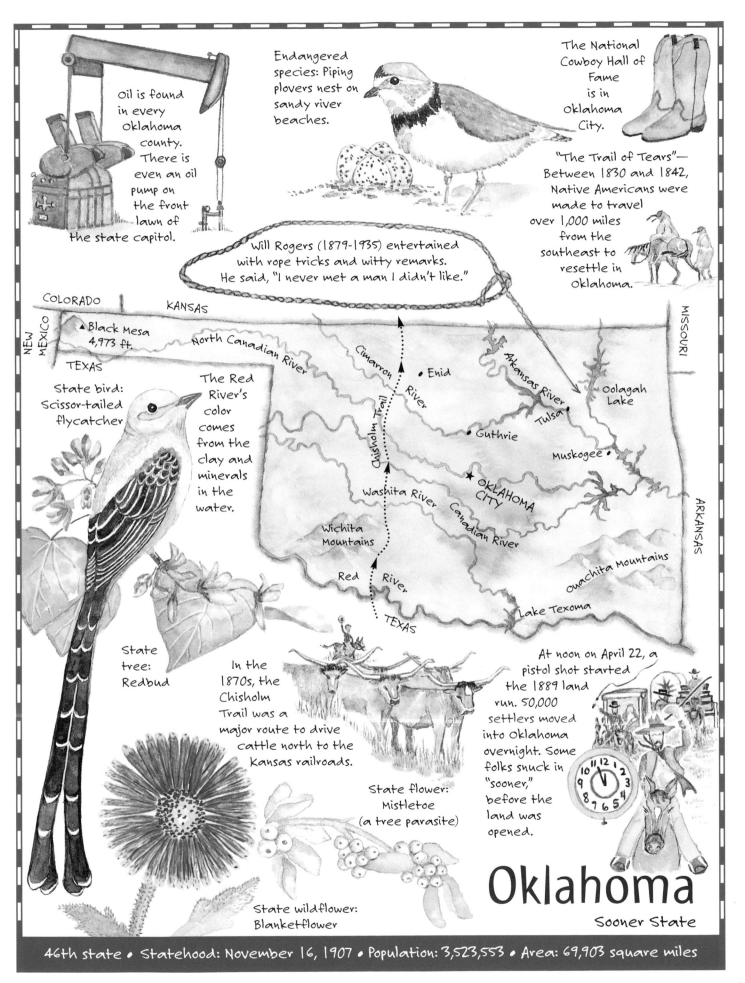

Oil is found in every Oklahoma county. There is even an oil pump on the front lawn of the state capitol.

Endangered species: Piping plovers nest on sandy river beaches.

The National Cowboy Hall of Fame is in Oklahoma City.

"The Trail of Tears"— Between 1830 and 1842, Native Americans were made to travel over 1,000 miles from the southeast to resettle in Oklahoma.

Will Rogers (1879-1935) entertained with rope tricks and witty remarks. He said, "I never met a man I didn't like."

COLORADO
KANSAS
NEW MEXICO
TEXAS
MISSOURI
ARKANSAS

▲ Black Mesa 4,973 ft.

North Canadian River

Cimarron River

• Enid

Arkansas River

Tulsa

Oolagah Lake

State bird: Scissor-tailed flycatcher

The Red River's color comes from the clay and minerals in the water.

Chisholm Trail

• Guthrie

Muskogee •

★ OKLAHOMA CITY

Washita River

Canadian River

Wichita Mountains

Ouachita Mountains

Red River

TEXAS

Lake Texoma

State tree: Redbud

In the 1870s, the Chisholm Trail was a major route to drive cattle north to the Kansas railroads.

At noon on April 22, a pistol shot started the 1889 land run. 50,000 settlers moved into Oklahoma overnight. Some folks snuck in "sooner," before the land was opened.

State flower: Mistletoe (a tree parasite)

State wildflower: Blanketflower

Oklahoma
Sooner State

46th state • Statehood: November 16, 1907 • Population: 3,523,553 • Area: 69,903 square miles

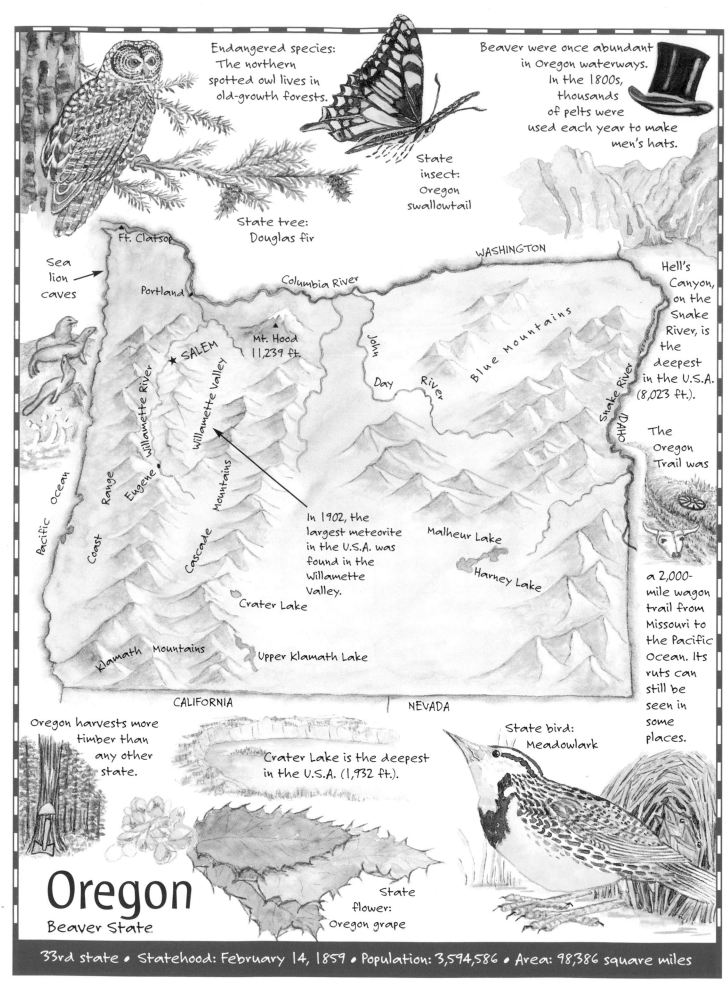

Endangered species:
The northern spotted owl lives in old-growth forests.

State insect:
Oregon swallowtail

Beaver were once abundant in Oregon waterways. In the 1800s, thousands of pelts were used each year to make men's hats.

State tree:
Douglas fir

Ft. Clatsop

Sea lion caves

WASHINGTON

Columbia River

Portland

Hell's Canyon, on the Snake River, is the deepest in the U.S.A. (8,023 ft.).

★ SALEM

Mt. Hood 11,239 ft.

Willamette River

Willamette Valley

John Day River

Blue Mountains

Snake River

IDAHO

Pacific Ocean

Coast Range

Eugene

Cascade Mountains

In 1902, the largest meteorite in the U.S.A. was found in the Willamette Valley.

Malheur Lake

Harney Lake

The Oregon Trail was a 2,000-mile wagon trail from Missouri to the Pacific Ocean. Its ruts can still be seen in some places.

Crater Lake

Klamath Mountains

Upper Klamath Lake

CALIFORNIA

NEVADA

Oregon harvests more timber than any other state.

Crater Lake is the deepest in the U.S.A. (1,932 ft.).

State bird:
Meadowlark

Oregon
Beaver State

State flower:
Oregon grape

33rd state • Statehood: February 14, 1859 • Population: 3,594,586 • Area: 98,386 square miles

42

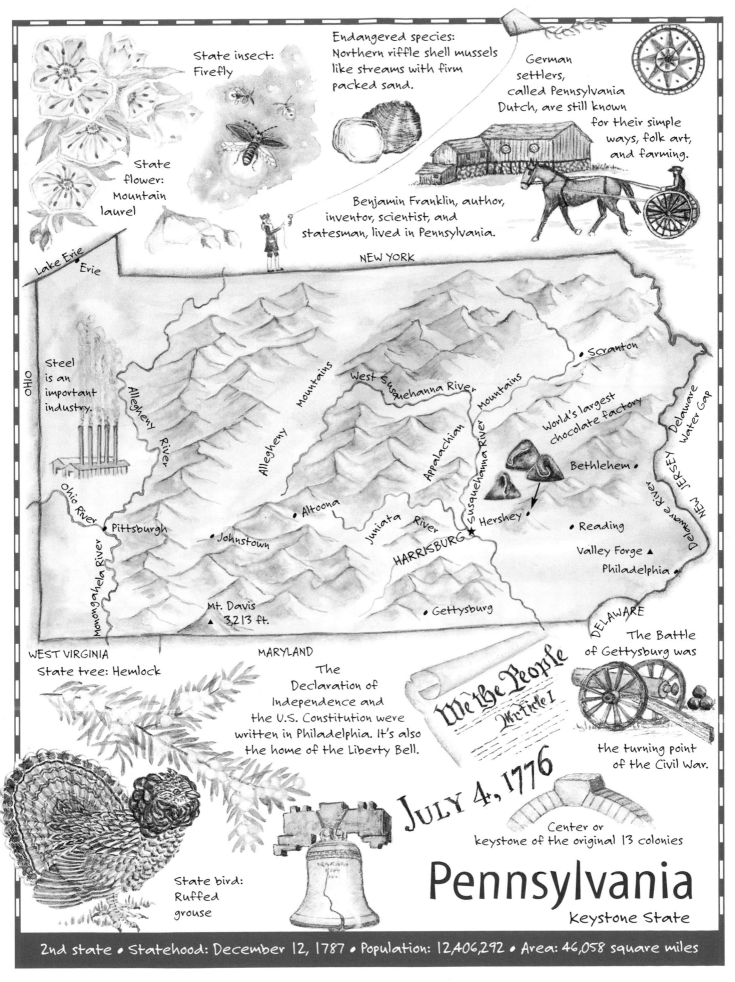

State insect: Firefly

Endangered species: Northern riffle shell mussels like streams with firm packed sand.

German settlers, called Pennsylvania Dutch, are still known for their simple ways, folk art, and farming.

State flower: Mountain laurel

Benjamin Franklin, author, inventor, scientist, and statesman, lived in Pennsylvania.

NEW YORK

Lake Erie
Erie

OHIO

Steel is an important industry.

Allegheny River

Allegheny Mountains

West Susquehanna River

Appalachian Mountains

Susquehanna River

Scranton

Delaware Water Gap

World's largest chocolate factory

Bethlehem

NEW JERSEY

Delaware River

Ohio River

Pittsburgh

Monongahela River

Johnstown

Altoona

Juniata River

HARRISBURG

Hershey

Reading

Valley Forge ▲

Philadelphia

Mt. Davis 3,213 ft.

Gettysburg

DELAWARE

The Battle of Gettysburg was

WEST VIRGINIA

MARYLAND

State tree: Hemlock

The Declaration of Independence and the U.S. Constitution were written in Philadelphia. It's also the home of the Liberty Bell.

We the People Article I

the turning point of the Civil War.

JULY 4, 1776

Center or keystone of the original 13 colonies

State bird: Ruffed grouse

Pennsylvania
Keystone State

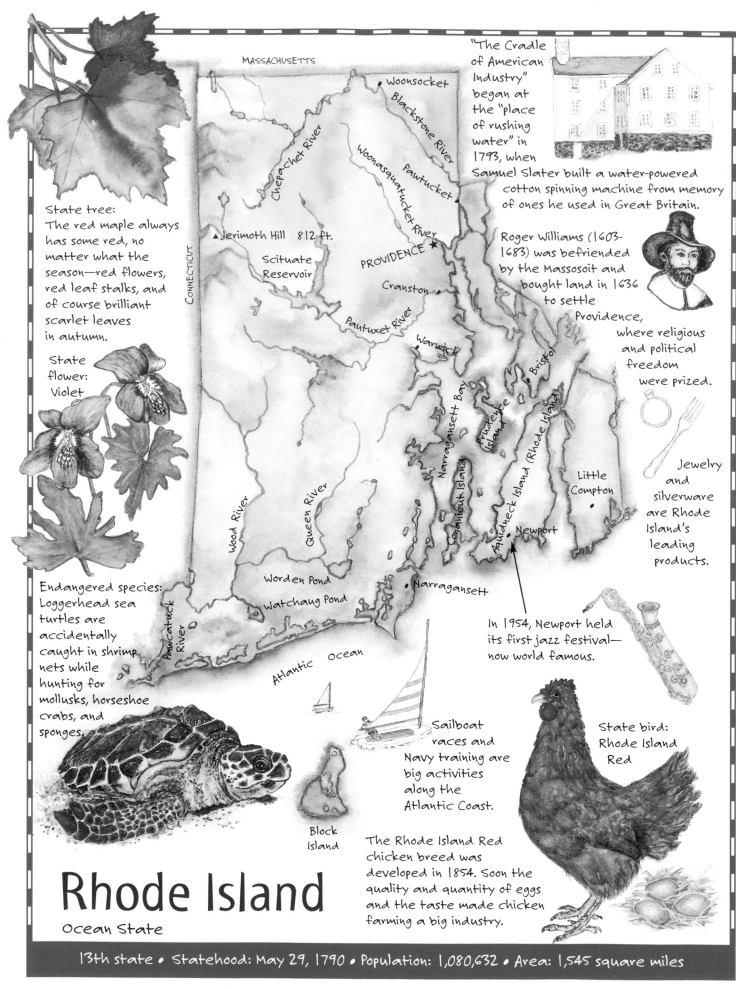

MASSACHUSETTS

Woonsocket

Blackstone River

Chepachet River

Woonasquatucket River

Pawtucket

▲ Jerimoth Hill 812 ft.

Scituate Reservoir

PROVIDENCE ★

Cranston

Pautuxet River

Warwick

CONNECTICUT

Wood River

Queen River

Worden Pond

Watchaug Pond

Pawcatuck River

Narragansett Bay

Prudence Island

Conanicut Island

Bristol

Aquidneck Island (Rhode Island)

Little Compton

Newport

Narragansett

Atlantic Ocean

Block Island

State tree:
The red maple always has some red, no matter what the season—red flowers, red leaf stalks, and of course brilliant scarlet leaves in autumn.

State flower:
Violet

Endangered species:
Loggerhead sea turtles are accidentally caught in shrimp nets while hunting for mollusks, horseshoe crabs, and sponges.

"The Cradle of American Industry" began at the "place of rushing water" in 1793, when Samuel Slater built a water-powered cotton spinning machine from memory of ones he used in Great Britain.

Roger Williams (1603-1683) was befriended by the Massosoit and bought land in 1636 to settle Providence, where religious and political freedom were prized.

Jewelry and silverware are Rhode Island's leading products.

In 1954, Newport held its first jazz festival—now world famous.

Sailboat races and Navy training are big activities along the Atlantic Coast.

State bird:
Rhode Island Red

The Rhode Island Red chicken breed was developed in 1854. Soon the quality and quantity of eggs and the taste made chicken farming a big industry.

Rhode Island

Ocean State

13th state • Statehood: May 29, 1790 • Population: 1,080,632 • Area: 1,545 square miles

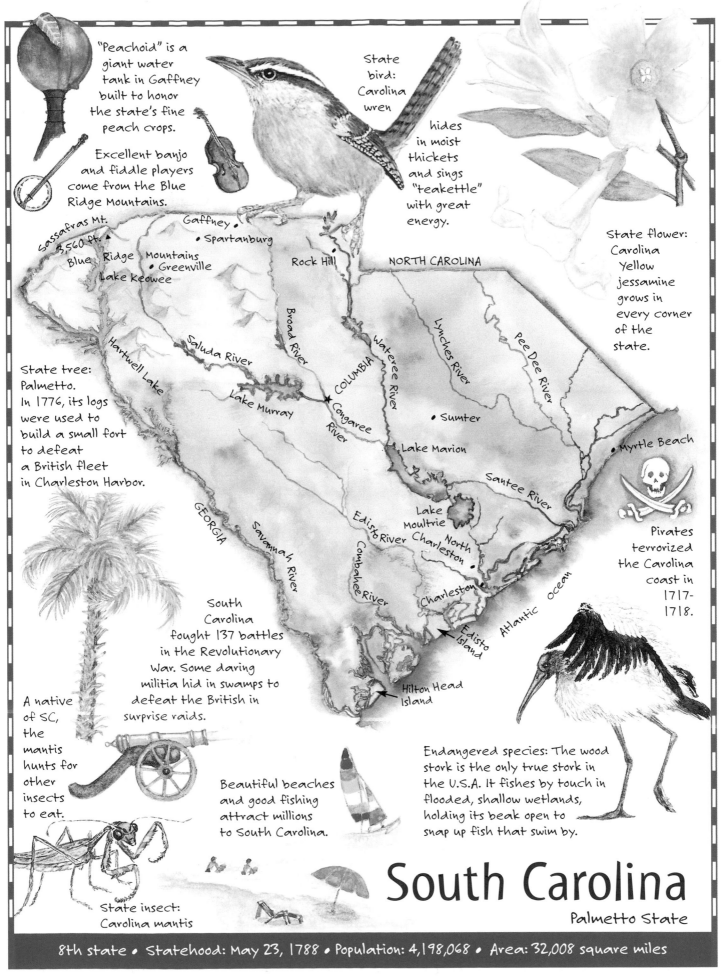

"Peachoid" is a giant water tank in Gaffney built to honor the state's fine peach crops.

Excellent banjo and fiddle players come from the Blue Ridge Mountains.

State bird: Carolina wren hides in moist thickets and sings "teakettle" with great energy.

State flower: Carolina Yellow jessamine grows in every corner of the state.

State tree: Palmetto. In 1776, its logs were used to build a small fort to defeat a British fleet in Charleston Harbor.

A native of SC, the mantis hunts for other insects to eat.

South Carolina fought 137 battles in the Revolutionary War. Some daring militia hid in swamps to defeat the British in surprise raids.

Beautiful beaches and good fishing attract millions to South Carolina.

Pirates terrorized the Carolina coast in 1717-1718.

Endangered species: The wood stork is the only true stork in the U.S.A. It fishes by touch in flooded, shallow wetlands, holding its beak open to snap up fish that swim by.

State insect: Carolina mantis

Sassafras Mt. 3,560 ft.
Gaffney
Spartanburg
Blue Ridge Mountains
Greenville
Lake Keowee
Rock Hill
NORTH CAROLINA
Hartwell Lake
Saluda River
Broad River
Wateree River
Lynches River
Pee Dee River
COLUMBIA
Lake Murray
Congaree River
Sumter
Lake Marion
Santee River
Myrtle Beach
GEORGIA
Savannah River
Edisto River
Combahee River
Lake Moultrie
Charleston
North Charleston
Charleston
Edisto Island
Atlantic Ocean
Hilton Head Island

South Carolina
Palmetto State

8th state • Statehood: May 23, 1788 • Population: 4,198,068 • Area: 32,008 square miles

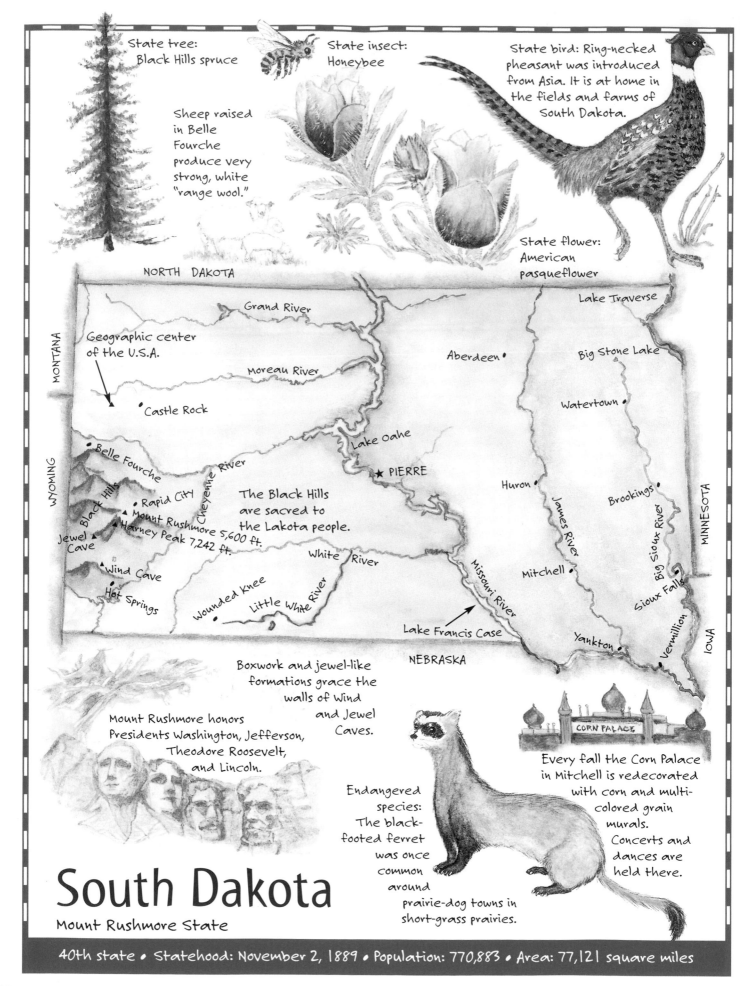

State tree: Black Hills spruce

State insect: Honeybee

State bird: Ring-necked pheasant was introduced from Asia. It is at home in the fields and farms of South Dakota.

Sheep raised in Belle Fourche produce very strong, white "range wool."

State flower: American pasqueflower

NORTH DAKOTA

Grand River

Lake Traverse

Geographic center of the U.S.A.

MONTANA

Moreau River

Aberdeen

Big Stone Lake

Castle Rock

Watertown

Belle Fourche

Lake Oahe

★ PIERRE

WYOMING

Black Hills

Rapid City

Cheyenne River

The Black Hills are sacred to the Lakota people.

Huron

Brookings

Jewel Cave

▲ Mount Rushmore 5,600 ft.
▲ Harney Peak 7,242 ft.

James River

MINNESOTA

▲ Wind Cave

White River

Mitchell

Big Sioux River

Hot Springs

Wounded Knee

Little White River

Missouri River

Sioux Falls

Lake Francis Case

Yankton

Vermillion

IOWA

NEBRASKA

Boxwork and jewel-like formations grace the walls of Wind and Jewel Caves.

Mount Rushmore honors Presidents Washington, Jefferson, Theodore Roosevelt, and Lincoln.

CORN PALACE

Every fall the Corn Palace in Mitchell is redecorated with corn and multi-colored grain murals. Concerts and dances are held there.

Endangered species: The black-footed ferret was once common around prairie-dog towns in short-grass prairies.

South Dakota
Mount Rushmore State

40th state • Statehood: November 2, 1889 • Population: 770,883 • Area: 77,121 square miles

State tree: Tulip-poplar

State bird: The mockingbird is a talented and varied singer in a state famous for different kinds of music: bluegrass, rock 'n' roll, blues, and country.

Davy Crockett was a frontiersman and a gifted storyteller. His motto was "Be always sure you're right—then go ahead."

(1786-1836)

In December 1811, a violent earthquake made the Mississippi River change course, and a giant wave created Reelfoot Lake.

State insects: Firefly and ladybug

KENTUCKY
VIRGINIA
MISSOURI
Reelfoot Lake
Cumberland River
Cumberland Mts.
Appalachian Mts.
ARKANSAS
Mississippi River
Tennessee River
NASHVILLE
Cumberland Plateau
Oak Ridge
Knoxville
Clingmans Dome 6,643 ft.
Great Smoky Mountains
NORTH CAROLINA
Shelbyville
Tennessee River
Memphis
Chattanooga
GEORGIA
MISSISSIPPI
ALABAMA

Endangered species: Spruce-fir moss spider. This tiny tarantula (1/10") lives only on moss-covered boulders in old-growth forests.

The Sunsphere Tower at Knoxville's 1982 World's Fair symbolized the fair's theme, "Energy Turns the World."

State flower: Iris

Tennessee walking horses are raised near Shelbyville and prized for their smooth gait.

State wildflower: The passionflower was the original state flower. In 1933, it was changed to the state wildflower.

Tennessee
Volunteer State

16th state • Statehood: June 1, 1796 • Population: 5,900,962 • Area: 42,146 square miles

State tree: Pecan

State bird: Mockingbird

Texas has many unusual animals. The armadillo protects itself with 9 tough armor bands that overlap.

On May 1, 1981, Henry Cisneros was sworn in as the first Hispanic mayor of a major U.S. city (San Antonio).

In spring, cactus blossoms fill the Texas deserts with color.

Texas leads the nation in raising beef cattle.

Canadian River

• Amarillo

• Lubbock

NEW MEXICO

El Paso

▲ Guadalupe Peak 8,751 ft.

Chisos Mountains

Pecos River

OKLAHOMA

Wichita Falls •

Red River

Fort Worth

• Abilene

Colorado River

Brazos River

Trinity River

Neches River

Texarkana

ARKANSAS

LOUISIANA

Sabine River

• Dallas

★ AUSTIN

Guadalupe River

Houston

Galveston

Water sports are popular on the Gulf Coast.

Endangered species: Whooping cranes are the tallest birds feeding in marshes.

MEXICO

Rio Grande

San Antonio •

Nueces River

Corpus Christi

Gulf of Mexico

Texas has a spicy influence from South of the Border.

State flower: Bluebonnet

In 1836, a small army defended a walled mission, the Alamo, in a battle of independence from Mexico. All were killed.

Texas leads all states in the production of oil.

The cry of the Texas Revolution was "Remember the Alamo."

Texas
Lone Star State

28th state • Statehood: December 29, 1845 • Population: 22,490,022 • Area: 268,601 square miles

48

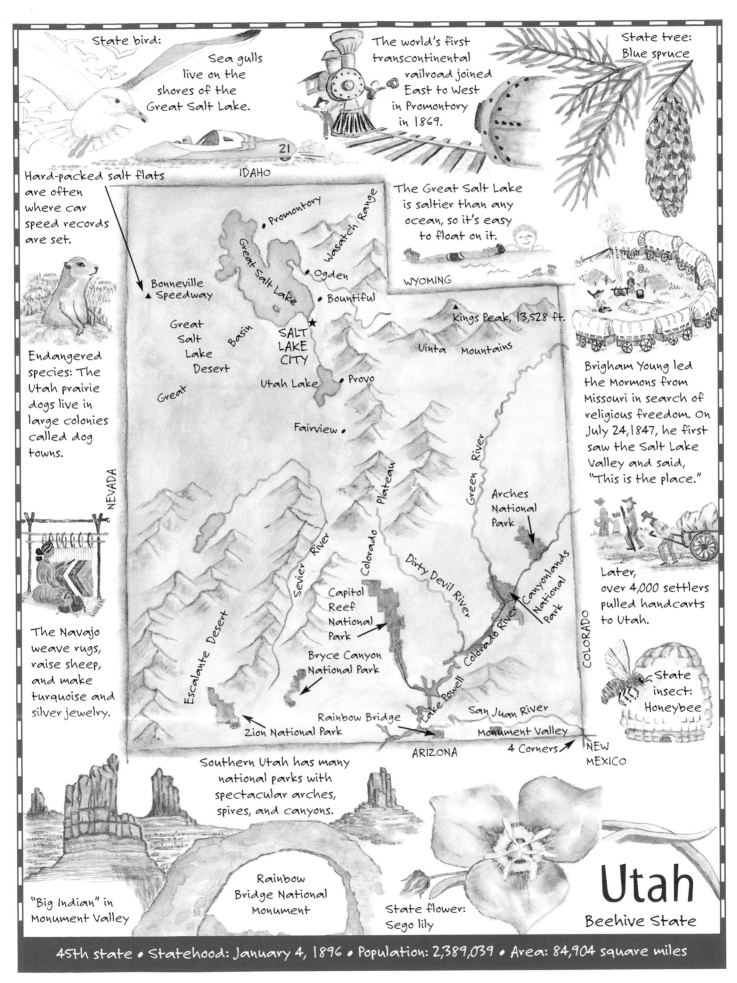

State bird: Sea gulls live on the shores of the Great Salt Lake.

The world's first transcontinental railroad joined East to West in Promontory in 1869.

State tree: Blue spruce

Hard-packed salt flats are often where car speed records are set.

The Great Salt Lake is saltier than any ocean, so it's easy to float on it.

Endangered species: The Utah prairie dogs live in large colonies called dog towns.

Brigham Young led the Mormons from Missouri in search of religious freedom. On July 24, 1847, he first saw the Salt Lake Valley and said, "This is the place."

The Navajo weave rugs, raise sheep, and make turquoise and silver jewelry.

Later, over 4,000 settlers pulled handcarts to Utah.

State insect: Honeybee

IDAHO

Promontory

Great Salt Lake

Wasatch Range

Ogden

Bountiful

Bonneville Speedway

Great Salt Lake Desert

Basin

Great

SALT LAKE CITY

Utah Lake

Provo

Fairview

Kings Peak, 13,528 ft.

Uinta Mountains

WYOMING

NEVADA

Sevier River

Escalante Desert

Plateau

Colorado

Capitol Reef National Park

Bryce Canyon National Park

Zion National Park

Rainbow Bridge

Dirty Devil River

Green River

Arches National Park

Canyonlands National Park

Colorado River

Lake Powell

San Juan River

Monument Valley

COLORADO

ARIZONA

4 Corners

NEW MEXICO

Southern Utah has many national parks with spectacular arches, spires, and canyons.

"Big Indian" in Monument Valley

Rainbow Bridge National Monument

State flower: Sego lily

Utah
Beehive State

45th state • Statehood: January 4, 1896 • Population: 2,389,039 • Area: 84,904 square miles

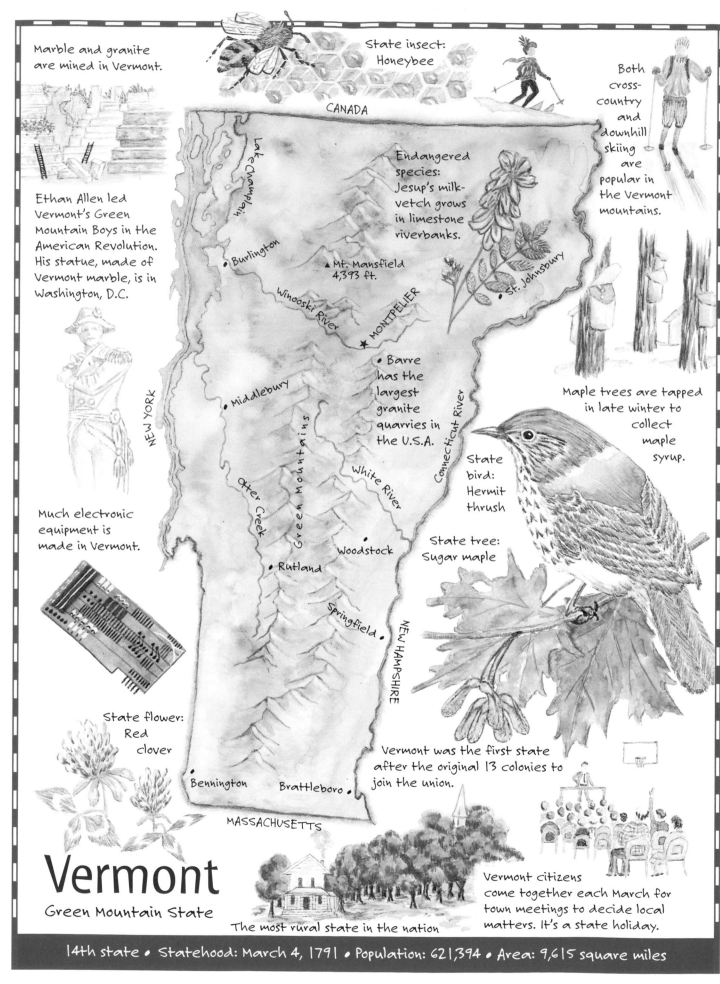

Marble and granite are mined in Vermont.

State insect: Honeybee

Both cross-country and downhill skiing are popular in the Vermont mountains.

CANADA

Ethan Allen led Vermont's Green Mountain Boys in the American Revolution. His statue, made of Vermont marble, is in Washington, D.C.

Endangered species: Jesup's milk-vetch grows in limestone riverbanks.

Lake Champlain

• Burlington

▲ Mt. Mansfield 4,393 ft.

Winooski River

MONTPELIER ★

• St. Johnsbury

Maple trees are tapped in late winter to collect maple syrup.

NEW YORK

• Barre has the largest granite quarries in the U.S.A.

• Middlebury

Green Mountains

Otter Creek

Connecticut River

White River

State bird: Hermit thrush

State tree: Sugar maple

Much electronic equipment is made in Vermont.

• Rutland

Woodstock •

Springfield •

NEW HAMPSHIRE

State flower: Red clover

• Bennington

Brattleboro •

Vermont was the first state after the original 13 colonies to join the union.

MASSACHUSETTS

Vermont

Green Mountain State

The most rural state in the nation

Vermont citizens come together each March for town meetings to decide local matters. It's a state holiday.

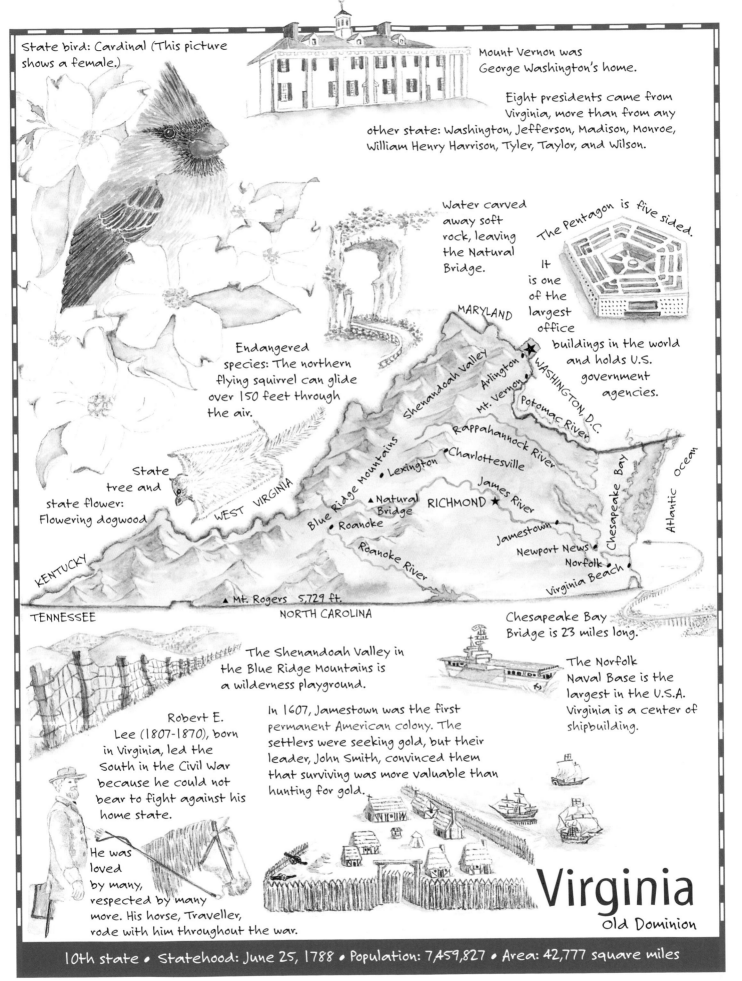

State bird: Cardinal (This picture shows a female.)

Mount Vernon was George Washington's home.

Eight presidents came from Virginia, more than from any other state: Washington, Jefferson, Madison, Monroe, William Henry Harrison, Tyler, Taylor, and Wilson.

Water carved away soft rock, leaving the Natural Bridge.

The Pentagon is five sided.

It is one of the largest office buildings in the world and holds U.S. government agencies.

Endangered species: The northern flying squirrel can glide over 150 feet through the air.

State tree and state flower: Flowering dogwood

MARYLAND

Shenandoah Valley

Arlington
WASHINGTON, D.C.
Mt. Vernon
Potomac River
Rappahannock River
Charlottesville
Lexington
Blue Ridge Mountains
Natural Bridge
RICHMOND
James River
Chesapeake Bay
Atlantic Ocean
Roanoke
Jamestown
Newport News
Norfolk
Virginia Beach
WEST VIRGINIA
Roanoke River

KENTUCKY

▲ Mt. Rogers 5,729 ft.

TENNESSEE

NORTH CAROLINA

Chesapeake Bay Bridge is 23 miles long.

The Shenandoah Valley in the Blue Ridge Mountains is a wilderness playground.

The Norfolk Naval Base is the largest in the U.S.A. Virginia is a center of shipbuilding.

Robert E. Lee (1807-1870), born in Virginia, led the South in the Civil War because he could not bear to fight against his home state.

In 1607, Jamestown was the first permanent American colony. The settlers were seeking gold, but their leader, John Smith, convinced them that surviving was more valuable than hunting for gold.

He was loved by many, respected by many more. His horse, Traveller, rode with him throughout the war.

Virginia
Old Dominion

10th state • Statehood: June 25, 1788 • Population: 7,459,827 • Area: 42,777 square miles

Washington grows more apples than anywhere else in the U.S.A.

Tacoma has the world's tallest totem pole, 105 feet high. Many Pacific Northwest tribes have family or clan emblems on their poles.

Endangered species: Olive ridley sea turtles mate in the Pacific Ocean.

State flower: Coast rhododendron love the rain-forest climate of western Washington.

CANADA

San Juan Islands

Strait of Juan de Fuca

Bellingham

Skagit River

Puget Sound

Olympic Mountains

Cascade Mountains

Wenatchee River

Lake Chelan

Okanogan River

Pend Oreille River

Rocky Mountains

Spokane River

IDAHO

Spokane

Grand Coulee Dam

Columbia Plateau

Pacific Ocean

Seattle

Tacoma

★OLYMPIA

Centralia

Wenatchee

Columbia River

Mt. Rainier 14,410 ft.

Mt. St. Helens erupted May 18, 1980, spitting ashes around the world.

Yakima

Yakima River

Snake River

Walla Walla

Vancouver

Columbia River

OREGON

The Space Needle, a tower in Seattle, is 607 feet high. An elevator takes people to see the view from the top.

State tree: Western hemlock and other evergreens cover half the state.

The only state named after a president

Sockeye and chinook salmon are born in freshwater rivers, swim to the ocean, and return to their birthplace to spawn.

State bird: Goldfinch. These "wild canaries" are found coast to coast.

Washington
Evergreen State

42nd state • Statehood: November 11, 1889 • Population: 6,203,788 • Area: 71,302 square miles

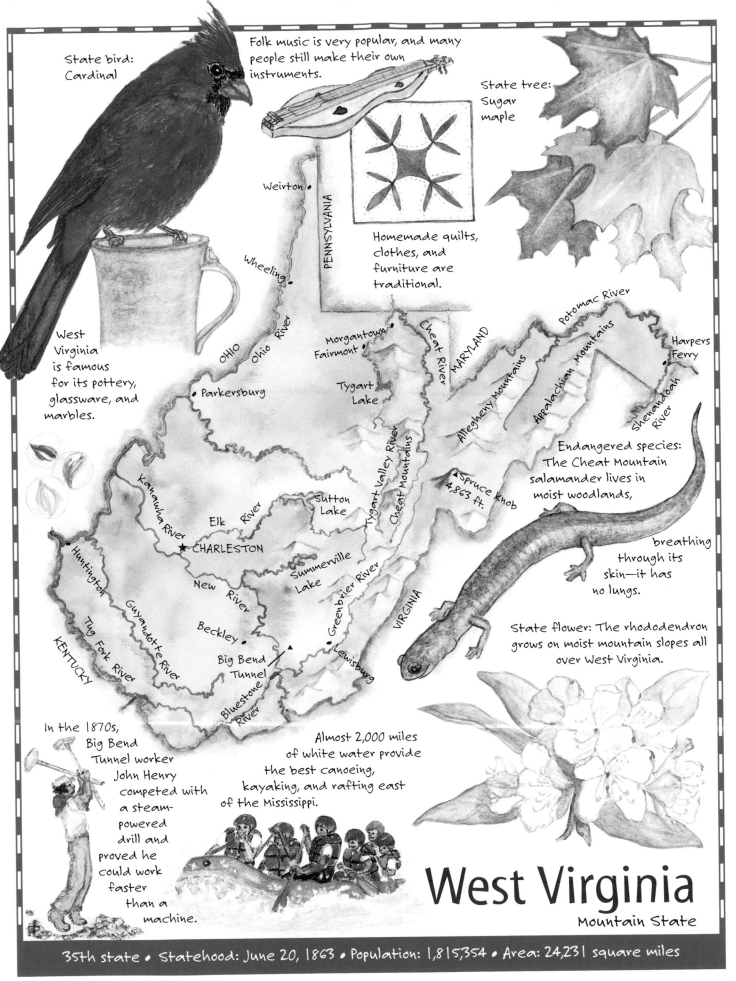

State bird: Cardinal

Folk music is very popular, and many people still make their own instruments.

State tree: Sugar maple

Homemade quilts, clothes, and furniture are traditional.

West Virginia is famous for its pottery, glassware, and marbles.

Weirton

PENNSYLVANIA

Wheeling

OHIO

Ohio River

Parkersburg

Morgantown
Fairmont

Cheat River

MARYLAND

Potomac River

Appalachian Mountains

Allegheny Mountains

Harpers Ferry

Shenandoah River

Tygart Lake

Tygart Valley River

Cheat Mountains

Spruce Knob 4,863 ft.

Endangered species: The Cheat Mountain salamander lives in moist woodlands,

Kanawha River

Elk River

Sutton Lake

CHARLESTON

breathing through its skin—it has no lungs.

Huntington

New River

Summerville Lake

Greenbrier River

VIRGINIA

Beckley

State flower: The rhododendron grows on moist mountain slopes all over West Virginia.

Guyandotte River

Tug Fork River

KENTUCKY

Big Bend Tunnel

Lewisburg

Bluestone River

In the 1870s, Big Bend Tunnel worker John Henry competed with a steam-powered drill and proved he could work faster than a machine.

Almost 2,000 miles of white water provide the best canoeing, kayaking, and rafting east of the Mississippi.

West Virginia
Mountain State

35th state • Statehood: June 20, 1863 • Population: 1,815,354 • Area: 24,231 square miles

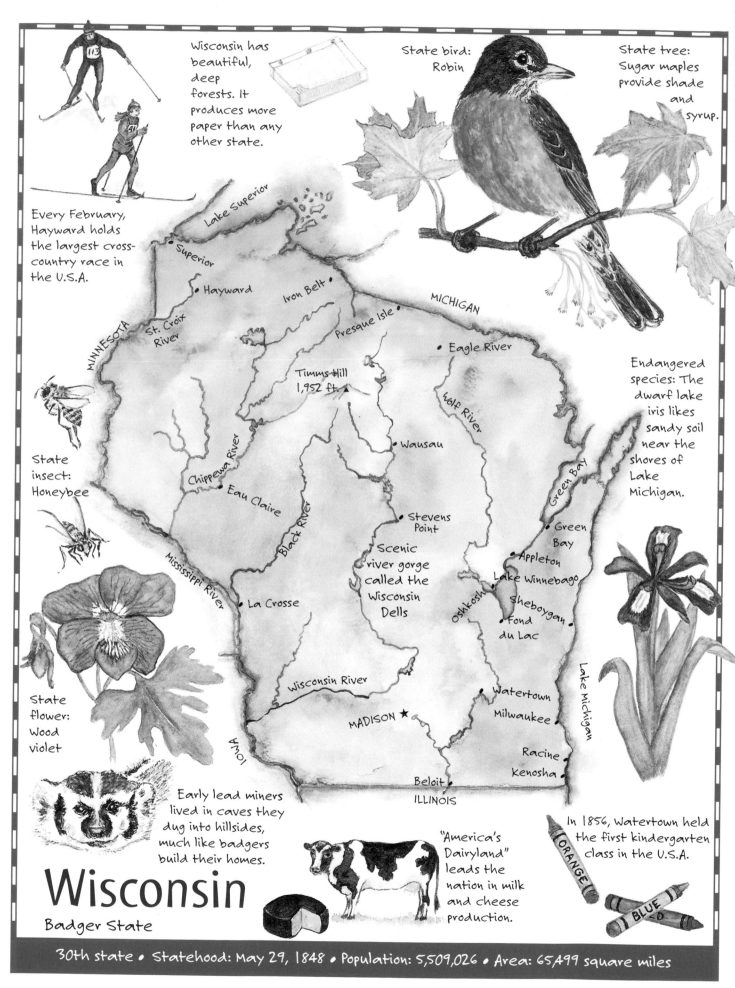

Wisconsin has beautiful, deep forests. It produces more paper than any other state.

State bird: Robin

State tree: Sugar maples provide shade and syrup.

Every February, Hayward holds the largest cross-country race in the U.S.A.

Lake Superior

Superior

Hayward

Iron Belt

MICHIGAN

MINNESOTA

St. Croix River

Presque Isle

Eagle River

Timms Hill 1,952 ft. ▲

Wolf River

State insect: Honeybee

Chippewa River

Eau Claire

Wausau

Black River

Stevens Point

Scenic river gorge called the Wisconsin Dells

Green Bay

Endangered species: The dwarf lake iris likes sandy soil near the shores of Lake Michigan.

Green Bay

Appleton

Lake Winnebago

Oshkosh

Sheboygan

Fond du Lac

Mississippi River

La Crosse

State flower: Wood violet

Wisconsin River

IOWA

MADISON ★

Watertown

Milwaukee

Lake Michigan

Racine

Kenosha

Beloit

ILLINOIS

Early lead miners lived in caves they dug into hillsides, much like badgers build their homes.

Wisconsin

Badger State

"America's Dairyland" leads the nation in milk and cheese production.

In 1856, Watertown held the first kindergarten class in the U.S.A.

ORANGE

BLUE

30th state • Statehood: May 29, 1848 • Population: 5,509,026 • Area: 65,499 square miles

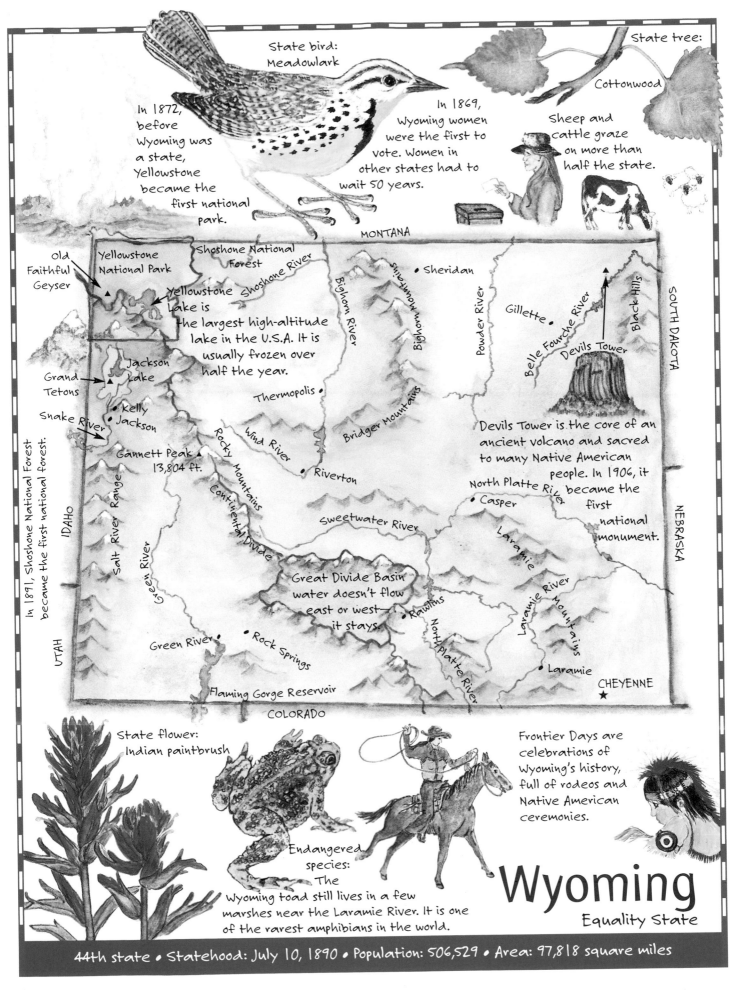

State bird: Meadowlark

State tree: Cottonwood

In 1872, before Wyoming was a state, Yellowstone became the first national park.

In 1869, Wyoming women were the first to vote. Women in other states had to wait 50 years.

Sheep and cattle graze on more than half the state.

MONTANA

Old Faithful Geyser

Yellowstone National Park

Shoshone National Forest

Shoshone River

Shoshone River

Sheridan

Yellowstone Lake is the largest high-altitude lake in the U.S.A. It is usually frozen over half the year.

Bighorn River

Shoshone Mountains

Bighorn

Powder River

Gillette

Belle Fourche River

Devils Tower

Black Hills

SOUTH DAKOTA

In 1891, Shoshone National Forest became the first national forest.

Grand Tetons

Jackson Lake

Snake River

Kelly

Jackson

Thermopolis

Wind River

Bridger Mountains

Gannett Peak ▲ 13,804 ft.

Rocky Mountains

Continental Divide

Riverton

Devils Tower is the core of an ancient volcano and sacred to many Native American people. In 1906, it became the first national monument.

North Platte River

Casper

IDAHO

Salt River Range

Green River

Sweetwater River

Laramie

Great Divide Basin water doesn't flow east or west— it stays.

Rawlins

North Platte River

Laramie River Mountains

NEBRASKA

UTAH

Green River

Rock Springs

Flaming Gorge Reservoir

Laramie

CHEYENNE ★

COLORADO

State flower: Indian paintbrush

Endangered species: The Wyoming toad still lives in a few marshes near the Laramie River. It is one of the rarest amphibians in the world.

Frontier Days are celebrations of Wyoming's history, full of rodeos and Native American ceremonies.

Wyoming
Equality State

44th state • Statehood: July 10, 1890 • Population: 506,529 • Area: 97,818 square miles

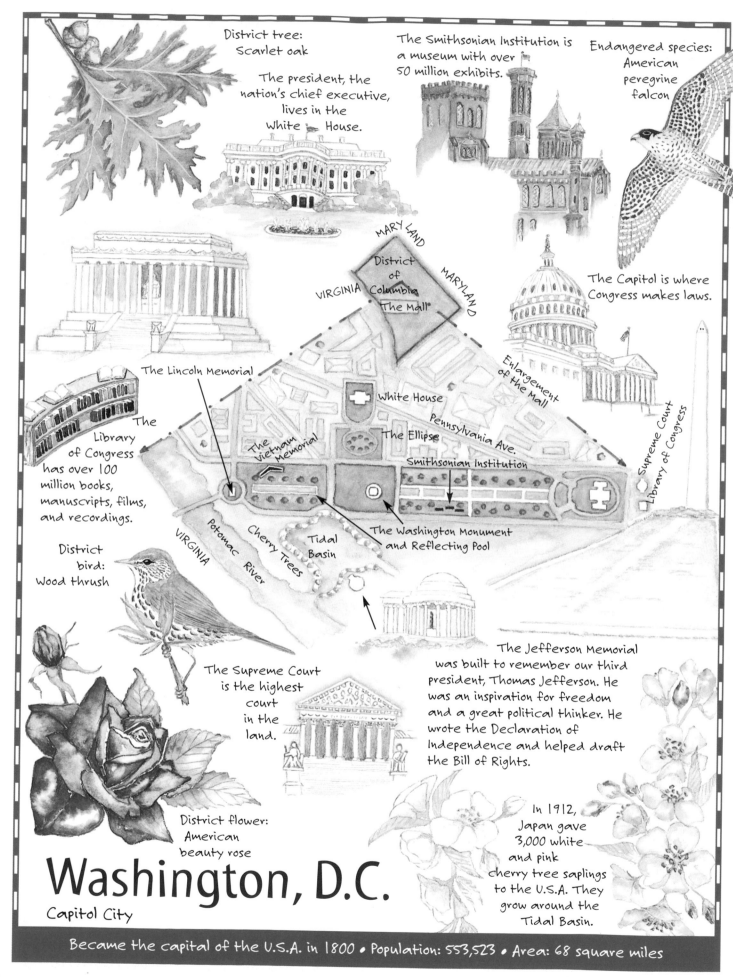

District tree: Scarlet oak

The Smithsonian Institution is a museum with over 50 million exhibits.

Endangered species: American peregrine falcon

The president, the nation's chief executive, lives in the White House.

The Capitol is where Congress makes laws.

MARYLAND
MARYLAND
VIRGINIA
District of Columbia
The Mall

Enlargement of the Mall

The Lincoln Memorial

The Library of Congress has over 100 million books, manuscripts, films, and recordings.

White House
Pennsylvania Ave.
The Ellipse
Smithsonian Institution
The Vietnam Memorial

Supreme Court
Library of Congress

The Washington Monument and Reflecting Pool

Potomac River
VIRGINIA
Cherry Trees
Tidal Basin

District bird: Wood thrush

The Supreme Court is the highest court in the land.

The Jefferson Memorial was built to remember our third president, Thomas Jefferson. He was an inspiration for freedom and a great political thinker. He wrote the Declaration of Independence and helped draft the Bill of Rights.

District flower: American beauty rose

Washington, D.C.
Capitol City

In 1912, Japan gave 3,000 white and pink cherry tree saplings to the U.S.A. They grow around the Tidal Basin.

Became the capital of the U.S.A. in 1800 • Population: 553,523 • Area: 68 square miles

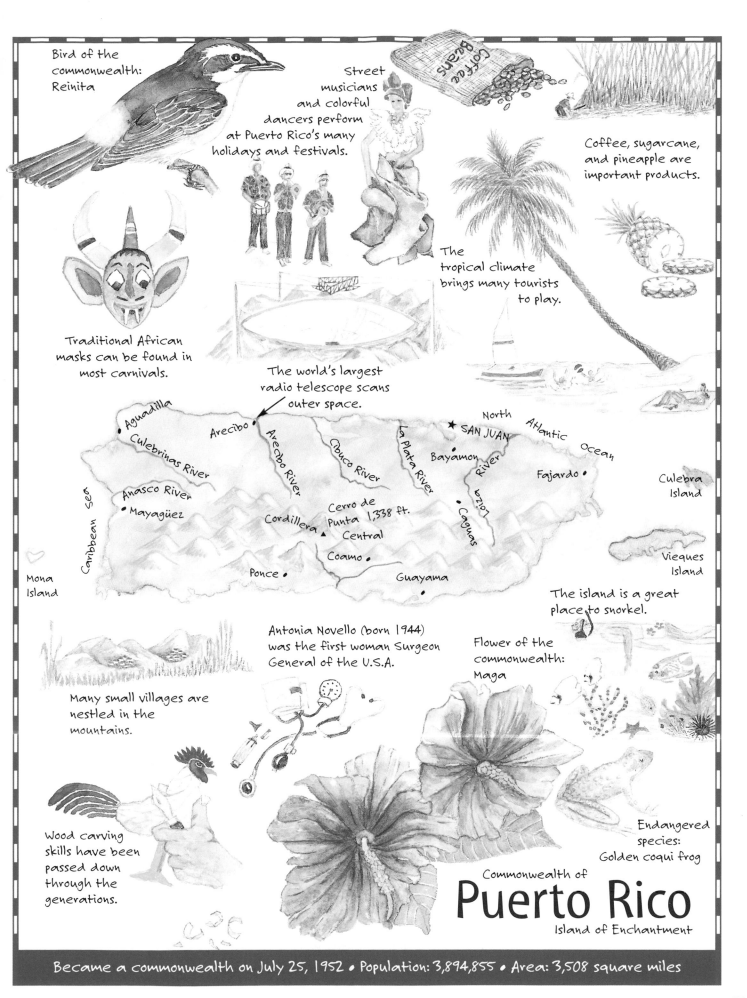

Bird of the commonwealth: Reinita

Street musicians and colorful dancers perform at Puerto Rico's many holidays and festivals.

Coffee, sugarcane, and pineapple are important products.

Traditional African masks can be found in most carnivals.

The tropical climate brings many tourists to play.

The world's largest radio telescope scans outer space.

Aguadilla
Arecibo
North Atlantic Ocean
★ SAN JUAN
Bayamon
La Plata River
Cibuco River
Arecibo River
Culebrinas River
Fajardo
Culebra Island
Caribbean Sea
Anasco River
Mayagüez
Cordillera
Cerro de Punta 1,338 ft.
Central
Caguas
Loiza River
Vieques Island
Mona Island
Coamo
Ponce
Guayama

The island is a great place to snorkel.

Many small villages are nestled in the mountains.

Antonia Novello (born 1944) was the first woman Surgeon General of the U.S.A.

Flower of the commonwealth: Maga

Wood carving skills have been passed down through the generations.

Endangered species: Golden coqui frog

Commonwealth of
Puerto Rico
Island of Enchantment

Became a commonwealth on July 25, 1952 • Population: 3,894,855 • Area: 3,508 square miles

"Old Glory," The United States of America

Alabama

Alaska

Connecticut

Delaware

Illinois

Indiana

Iowa

Kansas

Massachusetts

Michigan

Minnesota

Mississippi

New Hampshire

New Jersey

New Mexico

New York

Oregon

Pennsylvania

Rhode Island

South Carolina

Vermont

Virginia

Washington

West Virginia

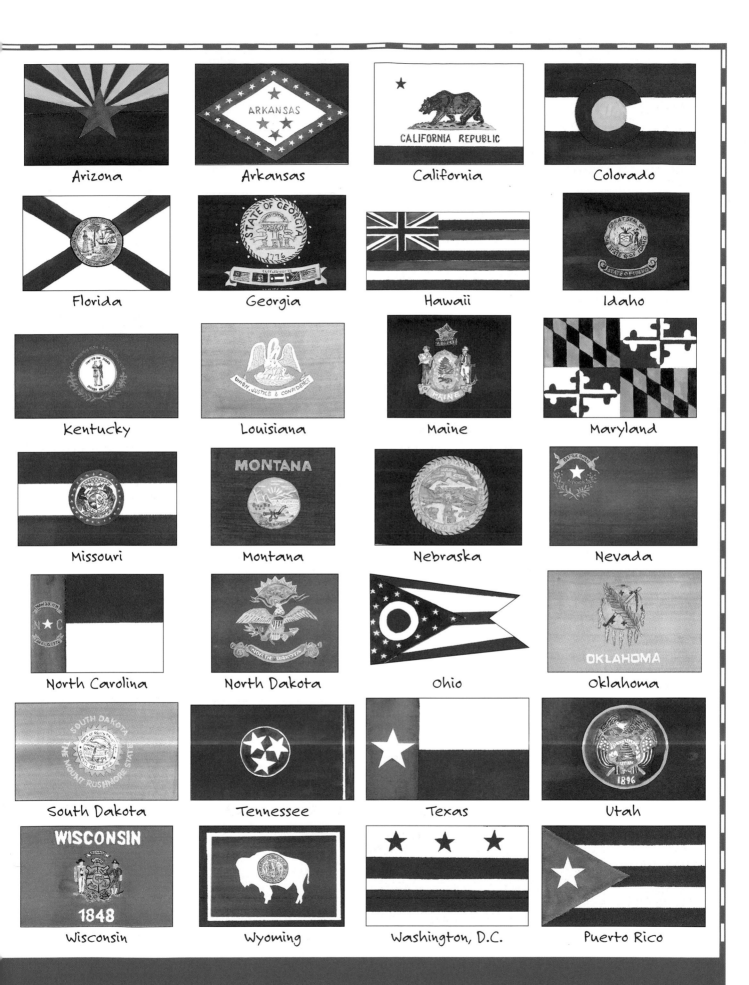

Arizona

Arkansas

California

Colorado

Florida

Georgia

Hawaii

Idaho

Kentucky

Louisiana

Maine

Maryland

Missouri

Montana

Nebraska

Nevada

North Carolina

North Dakota

Ohio

Oklahoma

South Dakota

Tennessee

Texas

Utah

Wisconsin

Wyoming

Washington, D.C.

Puerto Rico

INDEX

Technology and Innovations

Tourist Attractions

Transportation

War

Westward Expansion